▶ Children's Bodies in Schools

The Cultural and Social Foundations of Education

Series Editor: **A.G. Rud**, Distinguished Professor in the College of Education of Washington State University, USA.

The Palgrave Pivot series on the Cultural and Social Foundations of Education seeks to understand educational practices around the world through the interpretive lenses provided by the disciplines of philosophy, history, sociology, politics, and cultural studies. This series focuses on the following major themes: democracy and social justice, ethics, sustainability education, technology, and the imagination. It publishes the best current thinking on those topics, as well as reconsideration of historical figures and major thinkers in education.

Titles include:

Sue Ellen Henry
CHILDREN'S BODIES IN SCHOOLS
Corporeal Performances of Social Class

Clarence W. Joldersma
A LEVINASIAN ETHICS FOR EDUCATION'S COMMONPLACES
Between Calling and Inspiration

palgrave▶pivot

Children's Bodies in Schools: Corporeal Performances of Social Class

Sue Ellen Henry
Associate Professor of Education, Bucknell University, USA

palgrave
macmillan

CHILDREN'S BODIES IN SCHOOLS
Copyright © Sue Ellen Henry, 2014.

All rights reserved.

First published in 2014 by
PALGRAVE MACMILLAN®
in the United States—a division of St. Martin's Press LLC,
175 Fifth Avenue, New York, NY 10010.

Where this book is distributed in the UK, Europe and the rest of the world, this is by Palgrave Macmillan, a division of Macmillan Publishers Limited, registered in England, company number 785998, of Houndmills, Basingstoke, Hampshire RG21 6XS.

Palgrave Macmillan is the global academic imprint of the above companies and has companies and representatives throughout the world.

Palgrave® and Macmillan® are registered trademarks in the United States, the United Kingdom, Europe and other countries.

ISBN: 978-1-137-44264-2 EPUB
ISBN: 978-1-137-44263-5 PDF
ISBN: 978-1-137-44262-8 Hardback

Library of Congress Cataloging-in-Publication Data is available from the Library of Congress.

A catalogue record of the book is available from the British Library.

First edition: 2014

www.palgrave.com/pivot

DOI: 10.1057/9781137442635

Contents

Acknowledgments		vi
Series Editor's Preface		vii
1	Children's Bodies and Corporeal Expectations of Schooling	1
2	Social Class Inequities and the Body	24
3	Theoretical Frameworks for Understanding Social Class Corporeality	54
4	Corporeal Implications of Contemporary Schooling Practices	84
References		115
Index		128

Acknowledgments

I wish to thank:

- Bucknell University, for providing me a noncompetetive research leave in 2013–2014, during which the bulk of this writing and research was conducted;
- my students, who over the past 17 years, have never failed to enlighten and challenge me;
- my Writing Center partners: Peg Cronin, Sabrina Kirby, and most especially Deirdre O'Connor, who are superb conspirators and critics, always friendly, well-dressed, and kind;
- my friends, Mary Bushnell-Greiner, Bill Flack, Lynn Hoffman, Kathleen Knight-Abowitz, Jaxi Rothman, Roger Rothman, and many others, who graciously asked me how the writing was going and listened to the answer;
- my family, Mom, Dad, Peter, Auntie Judi, Uncle Ronell, Jacob, Ruby, and Benjamin, who somehow never fail to believe in me;
- my husband and the best "critical friend" I could ask for, Abe Feuerstein, with whom all things are possible.

Series Editor's Preface

Children learn both about and through explicit and hidden curriculums each day at school. Schools have been and still are contested sites for enacting social change as well as social reproduction. While schools most often are socially reproductive institutions, both social change and reproduction are transmitted and enacted through schooling and curricular offerings. So too, in explicit and in subtle ways, one's bodily manners, gestures, and comportment are moulded in schools. Description and analysis of the corporeal elements of teaching and learning in schools has not made its way into educational theory or practice until lately. Sue Ellen Henry's book is on the vanguard of such powerful social critique, using corporeal manifestations by students and teachers to understand educational practices and especially cultural reproduction in schools.

Henry grounds her inquiry in the work of Pierre Bourdieu and Annette Lareau. Bourdieu developed a social theory to analyze and assess how culture and, most importantly, social class are inscribed and made manifest in bodily habit and comportment. Henry uses Bourdieu's constructs with Lareau's recent work on child-rearing practice to highlight the importance of how bodily habit and comportment as well as linguistic competence and acuity are transmitted to the young or uninitiated in a culture. These practices are collectively a social game key to school success, which some play well due to internalization of cues and abundant social capital, while others barely succeed or fail. Henry notes that in schools, these social games of bodily comportment and linguistic competence are matched up to socioeconomic status, where poor or working-class students manifest different corporeal and linguistic habits than do middle- or upper-class students. The rub is that the game of succeeding in school is heavily weighted in favor of advantaged students, as the school and home for these students share similar linguistic and corporeal habits, practices, and norms.

In a brilliant section of the book where she uses categories of Lareau, Henry contrasts the "concerted cultivation" of advantaged students with the "accomplishment of natural growth" of less advantaged students. The logic of concerted cultivation maps well beyond the intimacy of the family to structured achievement arenas such as classrooms. The intimate and less formal family orientation and playful lassitude of the logic of natural growth may make those students happier or at least less stressed, but does not advantage them at school the way concerted cultivation does. As Henry points out, many teachers more easily privilege children of concerted cultivation over those others of natural growth and thus the achievement gap between the two groups only will widen.

Henry discusses two popular practices of current American schooling, Ruby Payne's curriculum for understanding students of poverty and the charter school organization, Knowledge is Power Program (KIPP). She shows how the regimented and controlled corporeal and linguistic practices advocated by Payne are similar to what is enacted in KIPP schools. She decries as inhumane the neoliberal shift toward producing human capital via the explicit linguistic and corporeal practices and norms that Payne's curriculum and KIPP schools promote.

The link between linguistic competence and school success is well known. Henry is right that "much educational research focuses on linguistic competence and the mastery of formal school language that facilitates social and academic success in school. Focus on children's bodies, however, remains embryonic." She presents us with a compelling and rich argument that corporeal performance and habit should be investigated by educational researchers much further.

A.G. Rud

1
Children's Bodies and Corporeal Expectations of Schooling

Abstract: *This chapter foregrounds the central question of the text: how are children's corporeal performances—shaped by their social class upbringing—interpreted by teachers and how might these (mis)interpretations influence the social reproductive effects of schooling? It asserts that important theoretical work of Pierre Bourdieu and Annette Lareau can help researchers understand the corporeal performances of children in different social class backgrounds. Self-control is explored as a central mechanism by which different corporeal performances become advantageous or detrimental in navigating the somatic expectations of school. This chapter concludes by arguing that neoliberal educational practices have detrimental consequences for children's development of authentic forms of self-control.*

Keywords: corporeal performance; self-control; social class

Henry, Sue Ellen. *Children's Bodies in Schools: Corporeal Performances of Social Class.* New York: Palgrave Macmillan, 2014. DOI: 10.1057/9781137442635.0004.

An invitation

What is your first or near-first memory of instruction on how to move your body in a particular way? Maybe your story comes from the world of sport, having a coach demonstrate the right way to throw a ball, run and kick simultaneously, or run backward. Perhaps a parent or family elder told you to "sit up at the table," or "chew with your mouth closed," or some other sort of instruction related to eating.

Or, perhaps your story takes place in school: a teacher giving a direct lesson on proper desk posture, hand position when holding a pencil, or appropriate position for reading. One of my most profound memories of instruction for the body occurred at school, but the lesson was given by my then dearest friend Meredith, in 7th grade. We were in the school cafeteria. Over our lunches of hamburger and tater tots, we talked about our days, and whether we were going to have a sleepover at her house that weekend. As lunch ended, we got up to empty our trash and return the trays to their cart. As I walked back to Meredith to go to our 5th period class, she conveyed something that even then I knew was important.

"You walk so heavy and swing your arms too much," Meredith critiqued. "Don't stomp and keep your arms at your sides, here, like this," she said, as she demonstrated the daintier, feminine gait that she thought was appropriate for all girls. Indeed, her walk did appear different from the way I felt my body moving when I walked. I walked with a distinct purpose, a direction, fast and focused. Meredith's walk was more graceful and gentle, aiming in a direction but not nearly as hurried and stiff as my gait. Meredith's instructions were jarring in their force. Her critique reminded me that I was visible and that others were watching. She framed the gendered and classed social environment in which I was operating at school and she gave me clear advice on how to participate more appropriately (expectedly) within it.

Such lessons are ubiquitous, particularly in school. This ubiquity has the paradoxical effect of concealing our awareness of the comprehensive impact of these lessons. The fact that teachers, parents, and other children are consistently giving feedback on corporeal presentation and performance has a puzzlingly persuasive influence on our consciousness of our bodies. The ways in which we move our bodies throughout our lives—the gestures we make, the way we hold our hands, our gait, our stance, our facial expressions—are the comprehensive expression of a lifetime of ordinary moments and points of feedback. As literary theorist

Kenneth Burke articulates with regard to the development of rhetorical skill, we might best think of how we corporeally move through the world as the totality of a life's persuasion rather the result of one key lesson. Corporeal performance grows over time not "through one particular address, but [through] a general body of identifications that owe their convincingness much more to trivial repetition and dull daily reinforcement..." (Burke 1969: 26). In other words, the lessons we receive about our comportment are extraordinary due to their ordinariness.

My important lesson from Meredith many years earlier was catalyzed in my mind after a day spent supervising elementary student teachers many years later. It was early September in a kindergarten classroom, in a school with a growing Latino population and 58% of the students on free and reduced lunch. The student teacher was leading the children in a typical morning meeting activity that included counting the number of days of school that had passed. The seasoned cooperating teacher, a white man in his mid-forties, drew a seat next to mine as we both watched the student teacher. He leaned over to me and claimed, "I can predict right now who is going to have to repeat kindergarten." The statement shocked me. "How?" I asked him. Aware that very little of the "treatment effect" of schooling had happened at this point in the year, that no standardized measures of reading or mathematics skill had been given, I was curious about his rationale. This veteran teacher explained his logic by noting how some children "knew" how to sit on the carpet during circle time, that some children were more skilled at raising hands to be called upon, and that some children in the class had proper pencil grip. Adding to his calculus, he noted that some children had come to school knowing the alphabet, some had letter-sound correspondence acumen, and some could even write their names. But he began his explanation by remarking on the qualities of children's bodies, and the children's differential capacity to control their bodies in school-appropriate ways. I recall leaving that day wondering how this teacher was *seeing* the children's bodies as indicative of academic capacities that were, ostensibly, to be learned at school.

My fascination with the ways children's bodies were interpreted by teachers was reinforced during another student teaching observation later that same year. This time, at the same school, the scene transpired in a fourth grade classroom. "Brandon,[1] come up here," commanded Mr. Coates, a white man in his late thirties, veteran fourth grade teacher, and part time football coach for the local middle school. Brandon was a quiet boy of about four-and-a-half feet tall, white, with dirty blonde hair and an oversized T-shirt hanging to his knees, displaying NASCAR driver Dale Earnhart's signature. "When I ask you to get to work, that's what I mean," Mr. Coates explained firmly. Brandon stared at the ground. "Look at me when I'm talking to you. If you don't look at me, I don't feel the respect I deserve. Stand up straight –in our school, you stand up straight and look people in the eye when they are talking. Got it?"

What did Brandon learn about his body from this interaction? Was he displaying a corporeal posture of respect consistent with expectations at his home? Was Mr. Coates' admonition to "look me in the eye" a requirement that was familiar to Brandon? Had Brandon intended to be "disrespectful" with the way he held his body, or was his corporeal code for respect just different from the corporeal expectation of school?

These questions initiated my interest in understanding more about how teachers interpret children's nonverbal, corporeal performances at school. What sorts of lessons about the body are embedded in the contemporary schooling experience for young learners? How are these lessons shaped by the corporeal learning children bring with them from their home child-rearing experiences? How does our (largely) middle-class teacher population perceive children who come to school with corporeal practices different from their own? This book theorizes on these questions in order to move children's bodies from the shadows to the spotlight. As a starting point, I map Pierre Bourdieu's theory of social class construction onto Annette Lareau's recent work exploring the social class nature of child-rearing practices to theorize on the corporeal consequences of such learning. Following this analysis, I examine the influence of neoliberalism on the contemporary context of schooling, and how this ideology shapes both educational practices and children's bodies in schools. To explore these linkages, I investigate the potential impact of Ruby Payne's pedagogical advice for teaching poor children and the more recent infiltration of "cultural interventionist" schooling organizations such as the Knowledge is Power Program, or KIPP (Shuffelton 2013: 300). These regimes, which have broad public appeal, also have important and largely hidden consequences on children's corporeal performances that merit consideration. This text looks at the ways in which a child's social class and home environment influence her corporeal performance. When she brings her class-based corporeal performance to school, what might happen? How might she be received by her likely middle-class teacher? How will her corporeal performances be evaluated against the likely unconscious standards of middle-class somatic expectations?

Readers will be reasonably asking about the place of race, gender, (dis)ability, and other identities that shape how people (literally) move throughout their lives. The question is an important one, and many authors have explored the corporeal experiences and performances of these identity markers.[2] In Chapter 2, I explore some recent research on children living in these identities. The larger aim of this text, however, is to extend the current theorizing on children's bodies and the identity marker of social class. Because social class is a powerful organizing structure in US society, separating it from other powerful influences is necessary to gain a fuller picture of the ways in which social class influences bodily performance and gestures. This is not to argue that individuals live *only* classed lives; indeed, as a post-structuralist, I believe that our identities are intersectional and contextually framed. While I acknowledge the important interactions between social class and other significant identity markers in the lived experience of children, my goal in this book is to flesh out the co-constructed relationship between corporeality and social class in children.

Social class and social reproduction theory

It almost goes without saying that social class is a pervasive factor that shapes individual and group experience in the United States (Domhoff 2013; Kraus, Piff, and Keltner 2011). Sociology has always been interested in understanding social inequality, how it is made, and the mechanisms that produce it (Ridgeway 2014), but studying social class or socioeconomic status is difficult. One challenge arises from the general assumptions that (1) the economic opportunity structure of the United States is an open one and (2) as a consequence, one's social class is determined by the choice of how hard one wants to work and how much delayed gratification one is willing to bear. Indeed, a 2005 study conducted by the *New York Times* revealed that 75% of those surveyed answered "yes" to the statement: Is it possible to start out poor, work hard, and become rich?" ("Graphic: How Class Works—New York Times" 2014). This assumption arises primarily from the notion that upward social mobility is common and likely, even though data suggest that this belief is dramatically overstated. Hertz (2006) documents in his report for the American

University Center for American Progress that children from the poorest 20% of US households have a slim 1% chance of moving into the top 5% of income earners. Moreover, Hertz's (2006) data conclude that for children from the middle 20% of US households, chances of moving up into the top 5% of income earners are less than 2%. The most likely scenario is that a child will remain at his current income bracket when he reaches adulthood (Hertz 2006). Many other studies reach similar conclusions (Isaacs 2014; State and Search 2014; Stiglitz 2013).

Why do Americans cling to the idea of social mobility in the face of data suggesting that the opposite is true? Much of the explanation can be found in the cherished American ideals of freedom, liberty, and democracy, all of which were ideological factors in the establishment of our comprehensive system of public education. As Benjamin Barber (1994) explores in his critical text, *An Aristocracy of Everyone*, the American public education system is rooted in the enduring hope that education can be a common feature among all citizens and the facet of social life that sponsors an equal contest between individuals who are wonderfully diverse from one another. As Barber (1992) observes, "[d]emocracy is less the enabler of education than education is the enabler of democracy" (14).

Conflicts that exist in sociology also confuse scholars working to sort out these predicaments. While the notions of socioeconomic status and social class are ubiquitous to social science research, sociologist Paul Kingston maintains that inequalities among individuals are not so much categorical as they are gradational. In his work *The Classless Society*, Kingston (2000) argues that "class structuration in America is weak: for the most part, groups of people having a common economic position do not share distinct, life-defining experiences" (Kingston 2000: 4). Thus, the common but misdirected faith in meritocracy and sociology's wrangling about whether class exists in American society often lead to the confused use of terms such as "socioeconomic status" and "social class."

Indeed, sociologists frequently use "socioeconomic status" and "social class" somewhat interchangeably. While similar, these terms emphasize different, yet complementary, components of social life. *Socioeconomic status* is typically measured through a combination of educational attainment, income level, and occupational position. Such measures are meant to articulate categorical distinctions among groups relative to material resources at their disposal. Social scientists interested in studying *social class* maintain that this construct gets at important components of people's lives that go beyond the measurement of sheer material resources (Kraus et al. 2011; Lareau 2003). These scholars see social class as a relative, self-evaluative term, important not only for understanding the impact of access to material resources, but also for explaining individual feelings, thoughts, and actions (Kraus et al. 2011). These researchers often utilize the object measures of socioeconomic status, while adding to the mix a measure of subjective social class status (Cohen et al. 2008). Combining subjective social class rank with the objective measure of socioeconomic status helps researchers link these categorical distinctions to other behavioral patterns, such as "living in different neighborhoods, belonging to different social clubs, attending different educational institutions, eating different kinds of foods, enjoying different forms of recreation, [and] wearing specific clothes" (Domhoff 1998 cited in Kraus et al. 2011: 1).

Sociologist and social theorist Pierre Bourdieu sees these behavioral patterns as important components in explaining how social class is passed onto subsequent generations and reified within the norms of social institutions. His theory of social reproduction, developed from extensive research conducted in France in the 1960s, asserts that cultural capital, habitus, and body hexis are central social structures that set norms for behavior and choices within social fields. I explore these concepts in detail in Chapter 2, but as an overview, Bourdieu defines cultural capital as the "general cultural background, knowledge, disposition, and skills that are passed from one generation to the next" (MacLeod 2008: 13). Bourdieu defines habitus as "a system of lasting, transposable dispositions which, integrating past experience, functions at every moment as a matrix of perceptions, appreciations, and actions" (Bourdieu 1977: 82–83). In essence, habitus works as an overarching system establishing norms and expectations for individuals, based on the social class status one inhabits. Body hexis refers to the embodiment and use of the body that arises from habitus and cultural capital. As Bourdieu writes, "[b]ody hexis speaks directly to the motor function, in the form of a pattern of postures that is both individual and systematic, because [the body] is linked to a whole system of techniques involving the body and tools..." (Bourdieu 1977: 87). Thus, for Bourdieu, social class is inscribed on the body and is directly related to the gestures, posture, and other bodily behaviors often thought of as arising unconsciously.

Bourdieu's research affirms that children in various social class positions inherit cultural capital aligned with that social class position. Children of upper-class parents experience forms of cultural capital consistent with dominant social institutions, such as school, which confirms unearned advantages in this social field. Children of working-class parents are at a disadvantage when attempting to use the cultural capital accrued in their home environments successfully at school (Giroux 2001). As MacLeod (2008) maintains, through the differential valuing of upper-class cultural capital and the systematic devaluing of working-class cultural capital, "schools reproduce social inequality, but by dealing in the currency of academic credentials, the educational system legitimates the entire process" thereby concealing it from critique (14).

Copious data demonstrate that social class is a powerful organizing construct that shapes children's experiences in the home and subsequent experiences in schools (Downey, Hippel, and Broh 2004; Duncan, Boisjoly, and Harris 2001; Lareau 2003; McLanahan 2004). Some studies emphasize occupational and educational differences among parents as key to explaining different child-rearing parenting practices (McLanahan 2004; Reardon 2011; Sirin 2005). Such studies typically examine the effects of differences in parental education on monitoring homework, teaching study skills, and reinforcing other "school readiness" behaviors. These studies explain the material differences that result from different levels of education and the correspondence of education with occupation. These factors are then thought to influence parental choices such as time spent with children, family size, age of parents at birth of their first child, and marital status and stability (Sherman and Harris 2012).

Another angle present in research exploring the influence of social class on parenting emphasizes the process of socialization and cultural norms present in families of different socioeconomic status and social class backgrounds. This theme was an early presence in sociological literature, largely due to sociologist Oscar Lewis' well-known "culture of poverty" thesis (Lewis 1963; 1975). Lewis' now largely disregarded theory maintained that poverty was "passed on" vis-à-vis parenting practices that de-emphasized a strong work ethic and cultivated other "dysfunctional [orientations to]...civic engagement, family formation, and individual self-confidence" (Sherman and Harris 2012: 63). While the original theory is seen as classist and racist, more contemporary work from the cultural norms point of view looks closely at the ways in which social structures such as schooling and societal parental support networks influence "working-class cultural understandings" of parenting (Sherman and Harris 2012: 63). As such, this orientation provides a more holistic view of parenting, emphasizing the values that are inculcated and reinforced by parents in lower status positions. Arguing that parental behaviors change rapidly over time (Hays 1996; Lareau 2003), studies from this position suggest that parenting logic is best understood in its cultural and historical contexts (Sherman and Harris 2012).

Present in both of these themes is a persistent focus on verbal language differences in children that correspond with their social class home life to explain school success or failure. Indeed, language differences among children of different social class backgrounds are widely studied and understood by educators as a key factor in explaining the academic achievement gap between wealthy and poor children (Bowey 1995; Hart and Risley 1995; Heath 1983; Sirin 2005; Walker, Greenwood, Hart, and Carta 1994; 2011). Such research typically points to the differences in language and vocabulary development that result from social class distinctions in exposure to "print-rich" environments, and experiences of parents reading to children. This work suggests that children's early performance on reading ability and linguistic competence in school is reliant upon their exposure to language that mirrors the ways in which language is used in academic settings, arguing that children of the middle and upper class are advantaged due to their early exposure and practice with normative linguistic expectations of school.

Much of this work capitalizes on Basil Bernstein's linguistic research (1973), which theorized that various forms of language use correspond with social class position. Among the middle class, Bernstein (1973) theorized, "speech becomes an object of special perceptual activity and a 'theoretical attitude' is developed toward the structural possibilities of sentence organization" (Bernstein 1973: 61). Bernstein labeled this "elaborated" language use, to indicate that this use extended the applicability of language from subjective subject matter and emphasized a "conceptual hierarchy for the organization of experience" (61). Bernstein further maintained that "lower working class" individuals used language in a "restricted" manner compared to their middle-class peers, a code that limited working-class individuals from expanding on subjects in their speech and "progressively orients the user to descriptive, rather than abstract, concepts" (Bernstein 1973: 61–62). Annette Lareau's (2003) more recent work also finds that language use in families differs based upon social class status. Her qualitative analysis reveals, among other trends, elaborate "word play" present in middle-class homes and the use of language to give behavioral directives more common in working-class homes.

Lareau's (2003) qualitative study of middle-class and working-class/poor families' orientations to parenting and child-rearing practices is grounded in Bourdieu's theory and extends beyond documenting linguistic differences to explaining differential school success. Her data demonstrate that in addition to material resource distinctions present in families of different socioeconomic status, two different "logics" of parenting strategy cohere around social class position. Middle-class families operate from the logic of "concerted cultivation," and see their primary role as raising their children to become self-possessed, assertive adults. Working-class and poor families utilize the logic of "accomplishment of natural growth," and see their responsibilities as securing safety and general care for children. Lareau (2003) asserts that these different logic positions have significant influence on how language is used in families, the organization of time in family home lives, and the perceptions of authority families have in relation to dominant social institutions such as schools. What she does not examine, however, is how children's corporeal performances are shaped as a result of these child-rearing practices. How, for instance, might the comportment of children raised in the logic of concerted cultivation be different from that of children raised in the logic of accomplishment of natural growth?

Extending these questions to the school situation, what might be some of the consequences for young learners who use their corporeal performances from home in the middle-class environment of school? It is here that the earlier vignette of Brandon re-emerges. How was Brandon's social class status manifest in his corporeal performance during the interaction with his teacher? How was the teacher's social class status and role power on display with his corporeal moves during the interaction? While we know that adults read other adults' nonverbal communication for cues about social class (Kraus and Keltner 2009; Kraus, Côté, and Keltner 2010), there are currently no direct data on how teachers read children's nonverbal communications for this kind of information.

For these reasons, researchers and educators need a durable theory of social class comportment, one that considers how corporeal performance in children is shaped by the experience of schooling. Utilizing Bourdieu's (1991) theoretical tools of habitus, cultural capital, and body hexis to theorize the class-embodied corporeal gestures practiced by young children in schools, I argue that the unexamined class-based corporeal expectations of educators, together with the somatic expectations present in the hidden and explicit curricula of school, collide to create a complicated, intersectional, somatic school experience for children. I maintain that this co-constitutive system can explain some of the reproductive effects of contemporary schooling.

Children's bodies in schools: the landscape of discipline and the importance of self-control

Direct study and theorizing about the body is associated with many disciplinary fields, notably sociology, critical psychology, and geography. Consistent between all of these various disciplinary frames is what Escobar (2007) has termed the post-structuralist "ontological turn" in social theory. This "turn" aims to foreground the understanding of individuals in their social environments as "assemblages" (Deleuze, Guattari, and Massumi 1987), which Escobar (2007) defines as "wholes whose properties emerge from the interactions between the parts; they can be any entity: interpersonal networks, cities, markets, nation-states, etc." (107). These assemblages arise from the mutual and reciprocal interaction of individuals and social environments upon one another. As Escobar (2006) summarizes: "the focus is on the objective, albeit historical processes of assembly through which a wide range of social entities, from persons to nation-states, come into being" (107).

Critical from this view for the study of the body is that there is action (both by institutional systems and individuals) within local fields that is not only emblematic of larger systems at work (e.g., social class) but which alters local expressions of these grand systems in social fields. As Escobar (2006) explains, "what exists is always a manifold of interacting sites that emerge within unfolding event-relations that include, of course, relations of force from inside and outside the site" (109). Such a position highlights dynamics of power within local sites, such as classrooms, acknowledging the nontraditional role of student power as a legitimate force, as well as the traditional sources of power in school such as the curriculum, school rules, and adult authority.

This framework serves as the foundation for much of the work on embodiment emerging from geography (Katz 2004), sociology (Skeggs 2004), and gender studies (Walkerdine 1990). From an embodiment point of view, the argument is that systems of power, such as social class, are inscribed on bodies, bodies that then use their agency to influence their lives. This "turn" affords other social groupings, such as social structure and institutions, like school, to have influence on individuals, while themselves also being changed in the process of shaping others. As such, this "ontological turn" reframes a longstanding dichotomy in sociology between structure and agency. As Escobar (2006) observes, assemblages offer an alternative to conventional thinking where power is rooted either in the influence of institutions (e.g., structural elements such as social class or schools) or the authority of individuals to act upon their world (e.g., individual agency). The body then, as the argument goes, serves as a platform for agency as well as a canvas upon which to view the consequences of social power impressed upon the individual. The body, from this viewpoint, becomes both a representation of, as well as a tool for, action.

Students bodies in schools

While no objective data exist on how teachers interpret the social class status of young children through corporeal performances, theory and data do exist on related questions of how children use their bodies in schools, the effects of being a child who is deemed lacking in "self-control," and the effects of common early elementary school rules meant to cultivate corporeal self-control in young children.

One powerful early study of children's bodies and social reproduction in the classroom is Ray Rist's (1970/2000) seminal work *Urban School: Factory of Failure*. For two-and-a-half years, Rist followed a group of black kindergarteners through their early schooling experience, observing closely the types of interactions these children and their families had with their teachers, noting the teacher-held beliefs about the children that resulted from these interactions, and documenting the ways in which teachers altered their instruction of these children as a result. In what is now a well-known idea about the power of self-fulfilling prophecies, Rist (1970/2000) concludes that "the reinforcement by the teacher of the characteristics in the children that she had perceived as leading to academic failure, may, in fact, have created the very conditions of student failure" (27). Important for our purposes are his findings on how teachers used information garnered from their observations of children's bodies, together with proximal data regarding the children's social class status, to make judgments about the cognitive and academic potential of these young learners.

Rist's (1970/2000) study offers a detailed view of the social class cues that teachers likely unconsciously use to interpret student behavior and assess students' academic potential. By the 8th day of the school year, the kindergarten teacher assigned children to one of three reading-skill-based tables, relying exclusively on non-academic data, including: (1) name of the child and the parents, address, phone number, age of the child, and whether the child had preschool experience; (2) a tentative list of all children in the classroom receiving public welfare funds, and (3) information resulting from an initial interview between the teacher, the child and the mother during the school registration period–a significant focus of which was gathering medical information on the child and administering a behavioral questionnaire that assessed parental concerns on issues such as "thumb-sucking, bed-wetting, loss of bowel control, lying, stealing, fighting, and laziness" (Rist 2000: 11). Information gathered from these sources is particularly focused on framing the teachers' impression of the students' social class status and her perception of the child's body.

Differential treatment and instruction related to a child's table assignment arose early on, with children at Table 1 designated by the teacher as classroom "leaders" and the children at Tables 2 and 3 as "having no idea what was going on in the classroom" (Rist 2000: 11). Rist (1970/2000) notes that the teacher kept physically close to the children at Table 1 and gave them classroom responsibilities such as taking notes to the office, leading the class in the Pledge of Allegiance, passing out materials for projects, and reading the weather calendar for the day.

As the teacher assigned seating arrangements for Tables 2 and 3, critical social class distinctions between the children came into view; physical appearance was the primary criterion for table assignments. "While the children at Table 1 were all dressed in clean clothes that were relatively new and pressed, most of the children at Table 2, and with only one exception at Table 3, were all quite poorly dressed. The clothes were old and often quite dirty" (Rist 2000: 11). Rist (2000) also observed that the children at Tables 2 and 3 frequently came to school with the odor of urine. Similarly, the condition of the children's hair was also telling. Those children assigned to Table 1 all had either short haircuts, "processed," and combed hair; children assigned to Tables 2 and 3 consistently had either matted or unprocessed hair.

Rist's (2000) "self-fulfilling prophecy" notion comes about as a result of the instructional consequences of the teacher's evaluations of these children. The teacher assigned each table a name: Table 1 was the Tigers; Table 2 was the Cardinals, Table 3 was the Clowns. The teacher then physically oriented her instruction toward the Tigers, called on students in the Tiger group more frequently, and focused significantly more disciplinary energy on students in the Cardinal and Clowns groups. In one corporeal example, Rist (2000) describes an interaction between the teacher and a female student in the Clown group, who often could not see the material the teacher wrote on the board, due to the table position in the classroom.

> Lilly stands up out of her seat. Mrs. Caplow asks Lilly what she wants. Lilly makes no verbal response to the question. Mrs. Caplow then says rather firmly to Lilly, "Sit down." Lilly does. However, Lilly sits down sideways in the chair (so she is still facing the teacher). Mrs. Caplow instructs Lilly to put her feet under the table. This Lilly does. Now she is facing directly away from the teacher and the blackboard where the teacher is demonstrating to the students how to print the letter, "O". (Rist 2000: 14)

Based upon the teacher's perception and interpretation of the children's social class status, as communicated through their physical appearance, the teacher made judgments about children's potential academic capacities. As Rist (2000) writes, "what becomes crucial in this discussion is to ascertain the basis upon which the teacher developed her criteria of 'fast learners' since there had been no formal testing of the children as to their academic potential or capacity for cognitive development" (11). Rist (2000) maintains that the teacher, a self-described, middle-class person, used her own class-based notions of "fast learners" to shape her impressions of the children, thus inscribing into the classroom corporeal expectations and instructional modalities forms of cultural capital she valued and which she saw in the children she assigned to Table 1.

> Those who possessed these particular characteristics were expected to succeed while those who did not could be expected not to succeed. Highly prized middle-class status for the child in the classroom was attained by demonstrating ease of interaction among adults; high degree of verbalization in Standard American English; the ability to become a leader; a neat and clean appearance; coming from a family that is educated, employed, living together, and interested in the child; and the ability to participate well as a member of a group. (Rist 2000: 13)

Through this differentiated valuation of bodily performance, the teacher unwillingly advanced the process of social reproduction.

In another study drawn from the field of children's studies, well-known theorist Allison James utilizes post-structuralist thinking to understand children's bodies in the context of school. She views children's bodies as a form of embodiment; the corporeal accounting for the inscriptions that are made upon children's bodies that result from interactions with larger social networks and institutions, as well as the ways that children's actions (i.e., their agency) influence the contexts in which they live. Understanding the components of childhood as assemblages that represent the structures children experience as well as individual-level influences of the child and her body, James (2000) observes, "the concept of embodiment emphasizes, then, the situated agency of the body and a view of the body as not divorced from the conscious, thinking and intentional mind" (27).

James puts these ideas to work in her research on four to nine year olds in England. In her observations and interviews with children, James reveals the complex forms of corporeal agency children practice. Her data also exemplify the ways in which cultural features, such as stereotyping, become inscribed in children's minds and bodies. James (2000) maintains that children's notions of "normal bodies" "provide a measure of any individual child's conformity to that category" and as such, informs the child about his own self (27). This interactive process helps the child "develop a consciousness of the self as an individual and as an individual child" (James 2000: 27). James' data suggest that this process occurs vis-à-vis the inherent comparison between children that takes place in schools, produced not only by teacher's comments but practiced by children as well. "In school, structured as it is around age-classes, the same aged bodies may be smaller, bigger, or of equivalent size, with each variation providing a differential reference point for the child's own bodily sense of self" (James 2000: 28).

These frequent comparisons lead children to use their bodies to alter how others read their bodies, a common feature among childrens' corporeality (Skattebol 2006). She quotes from her fieldnotes a short vignette featuring Jerry, a rather small boy for his age. "Jerry,...bespectacled and bookish, gambled daringly with his body. One afternoon, self-deprecatingly, he described himself to the other, more laddish boys as a 'titchy little boring person' and thus forestalled their use of his body as a target for ridicule" (James 2000: 29). Critical here is seeing Jerry as an actor in his world, using his body as a tool of self-preservation and revealing his embodied knowledge that his body requires defense in the sometimes ruthless environment that is early classroom life.

Another important component in the embodiment of childhood and schooling that James' research suggests is related to the notion of developing self-control of the body. James' data reveal that early on in their schooling experience, children demonstrate their apprehension of negative stereotypical thinking about fat bodies. They exhibit their awareness of fatness "as a body characteristic [that is] based on considered and careful observation of the body in its social context," through the reasons they give for why being fat is "bad" – "you can't walk properly, you won't be able to run fast" (James 2000: 31). This early idea of the negative consequences of a fat body are related, James (2000) asserts, to the considerable emphasis in elementary education on developing and displaying corporeal self-control. "Through their experience in the school classroom children get to know that an acceptable body must be controlled and seen to be controllable: teachers exhort children to 'walk properly' just as often as they insist that they must 'sit up straight' and refrain from fidgeting" (31–32). This context reframes students' earlier practical reasons for the difficulties that accompany a fat body from mere practicalities to the more pressing problem of the absence of self-control.

Indeed, omissions of self-control and their bodily representations were frequently invoked by children to explain transgressions of other students, such as bullying and unexpected gendered behavior (James 1993). For example, after reading a story about bullying, one male student maintained that the bully in the tale was fat, when in fact, no mention of the bully's body had been made. Another example occurred with a young girl, Elaine, whose assertive, dominant personality conflicted with others' gendered expectations of girls. After a series of experiences over the course of the school year, one young female student remarked to James that Elaine's hands were "hard" and that Elaine was stronger than most boys in the class (James 2000).

As these examples suggest, the body works and is "worked on" (Featherstone, Hepworth, and Turner 1991) in multiple ways in classrooms. Much of this work involves children's influences on each other. As James (2000) notes, "[children] learn to perform a rather different kind of body work centered on the momentary and changing presentation of the body—its actions and its appearances...this kind of body work...takes place largely among the social body of children" (30–31).

The hidden curriculum of self-control in schools is especially critical to understanding the mechanisms by which some children's bodies become sites for social inequality vis-à-vis their social class status and the cultural capital they attempt to use. Sociologist Katherine Mason (2013) maintains that the attribution of self-control, and the lack thereof, is the means by which certain bodies become esteemed and others maligned. Self-control—it's provenance by those in situations of social power whose bodies meet normative expectations—is a critical mechanism for explaining which bodies experience inequality. Mason (2013) observes that the co-constitutive nature of social inequality and the body is based upon "moral and scientific discourses that value civilization, self-discipline, and restraint [and] bestow an aura of legitimacy—and full personhood—upon those in positions of greater power and privilege" (694). While in classrooms, young children are rarely in official positions of power and privilege, work in sociology of the body emphasizes attending to the subtle ways children use their bodies to gain power and focuses on the corporeal consequences of teacher-led demands for self-control.

Lessons about the body in school come from multiple places, with different emphases about their rationale and importance. Such lessons are ubiquitous in elementary schools, where children receive abundant feedback (direct and indirect) about the quality of their minds and academic work and the quality(ies) of their bodies. Any casual observer of the early elementary classroom will see that children's bodies are a prime location for commentary. Countless "transition" songs are sung by teachers to and with students affording young students a chance to "get the wiggles out." Accordingly, common rules of early elementary classrooms include ample evidence for the need to control students' bodies: keep hands to yourself; leave your seat only when necessary; be quiet in the hallways, raise your hand before speaking; stay in line. While sociologists of the body suggest that all people are subject to powerful messages about the body in public life, this situation is amplified for students in early elementary school. These tacit corporeal expectations are significantly influenced by social class norms and concealed from critique based upon the uncritical certitude teachers and administrators experience when enforcing cooperation from children. Indeed, the widespread aim to help young children develop corporeal self-control in pervasively classed ways may prove to be a powerful apparatus of social reproduction of the American public school.[3]

And yet, the work of school is ostensibly focused on children's minds, indeed often in such a way that the body is frequently cast as a impediment to "good" thinking (Jones 2000; Tough 2012; Watkins 2012). This situation is one that sociologist of the body Chris Shilling calls the body's "absent presence": the body is there, but not there (Shilling 2003: 17). Common elementary school rules suggest that in order to get the most from our brains, our bodies need to move and coordinate in certain prescribed ways. When the body is working properly, the rules promise, the body disappears from the learning situation so that the mind can do its work. As such, these practices construct children's bodies in an *abstracted* manner—that is, children's bodies become amputated from their brains and minds. Contemporary elementary rules for schooling, therefore, make children's bodies objects of social control by the teacher as well as mechanisms for communicating the low status position of the body within an existing power structure, aimed at creating narrowly "academic" minds capable of high achievement on standardized assessments.

Neoliberalism and schooled bodies

This bifurcation between the body and the mind can also be linked to the neoliberal influence on educational practices, which emphasize the necessity of creating individuals with capacities to further the economic security of their nation. Starting in the 1980s throughout developed nations, neoliberal economics infused into neoliberal politics and other public domains such as education and religion (Harvey 2007). The neoliberal stance on education is that the purpose of schools is to foster human capital, thereby ensuring the nation's economic power and individual success (Weis, McCarthy, and Dimitriadis 2006). Corporate discourses in education abound, including intense focusing on accountability, ensuring global competetive advantage vis-à-vis education, and heeding market forces in shaping educational priorities around "choice" (McGregor 2009). Indeed, neoliberal appeals in education aimed at constructing human capital serve as the "moral and scientific discourse" (Mason 2013: 694) upon which the production of self-controlled student bodies is predicated (McGregor 2009). Employing new managerially-focused systems for the purpose of maximizing the development of human capital is now ubiquitous in the education systems of industrialized nations and has become a central tenet of education policy. One example of the powerful influence of neoliberalism in education comes from the Organisation for Economic Co-operation and Development (OECD), which has recently codified the strong link between education and economic development in its 2011 "Skills Strategy" document, meant to help participating nations utilize public education dollars in efficient, economically-viable ways. According to the OECD:

> In a context of high unemployment following the crisis and increased global competition, ensuring an adequate supply of skills, maximising their use and optimising further development of skills in the workforce is key to boosting employment and economic growth.... Skills are thus high on the agenda, nationally and internationally.... this is precisely the time when investment in skills is most necessary to boost economic growth and facilitate the (re)integration of individuals into the labour market. Governments must ensure that expenditures on skills formation are efficient and effective.... (Organization of Economic Co-operation and Development 2011: 3)

This statement makes clear the importance of education in national strategies to develop a quality, skilled workforce for the global age.

Efforts to link the development of human capital in children to evaluations of the teachers who teach them is another feature of neoliberalism's influence in education. Students are not suffering alone under this regime; teachers' capacity for creative, original professional judgment is under deep threat. A powerful example of the neoliberal impact on teachers can be seen in recent Massachusetts educators' activism against "data walls"—the classroom posting of student's names and scores on assignments in hierarchical order—as a means of promoting greater motivation for superior grades ("Massachusetts Teachers Aim To Knock Down 'Data Walls'" 2014).

Practices such as this, aimed at differentiating and motivating students through competition, are common. McGregor (2009) suggests that the use of tactics such as the "data wall" and other forms of control and surveillance in schools, all in the name of cultivating the human capital of the student (body), dehumanizes students through its narrow assertion of the purpose of education. "Whilst it is true that training for livelihood is a vitally necessary *part* of education, it should not [be] the *whole*...Such an education dehumanizes young people, qualifies their 'value' in economic terms and ignores the multidimensionality of their needs as complex social and emotional, developing human beings...(356). McGregor (2009) further asserts that students seeking education for purposes other than serving future corporate masters are frequently labeled "subaltern" and deemed by schools as "troublemakers".

Use of tactics like the data wall fosters further segregation between students' minds and their bodies, equating education with control of the mind such that a compliant body is formed:

> Neo-liberals are critical of existing definitions of important knowledge, especially that knowledge that has no connections to what are seen as economic goals and needs. They want creative and enterprising (but still obedient) workers. Flexibility and obedience go hand in hand here.... a creative and critical polytechnic education that combines 'head, heart, and hand' is not sponsored by neo-liberals. The possible space for that discussion is closed down by an emphasis on an education whose role is primarily (and sometimes only) economic. (Weis et al. 2006: 247)

By limiting the benefits of education to capitalist aims, neoliberal policy in education maintains a separation between body and mind, offering a distinct opportunity to oppress the body for the purposes of the mind and advancing economic superiority. Indeed, sociologist of the body Kate Cregan (2006) maintains that this abstraction of bodies in neoliberalism arises in societies and cultures experiencing the undulating shifts from tribal to traditional, modern to postmodern "social formations" (4). She defines abstraction as "a lifting away from and re-presentation or reconstituting reinterpretation, of embodiment" (4). Cregan (2006) summarizes the impact of this abstraction of body and mind in four theoretical principles of embodiment:

1. We relate to each other as social beings through our embodied being, and the fact of our social interrelationships shapes the way we constitute our embodied being.
2. Different societies, different cultures, constitute embodiment in fundamentally different ways.
3. As social formations change over time, the settings in which bodies are lived layer more abstract disembodied relations over more immediately experienced embodied relations. Importantly, however, that does not mean that our prior understanding of embodiment disappears: different "embodiments" can and do co-exist, albeit in tension.
4. Those shifts, and the intensification of the processes of abstraction, are related to wider shifts in interpretations of the physical world and our relation to it, which in turn lead to an intensification of the rationalisation (the body as particularised, divisible object) and commodification (the body as property) of embodiment (5–6).

Importantly, ideas 3 and 4 reinforce the notion that power relations in society and social institutions are shaped by forces both within those institutions (e.g., role assignments in schools) as well as factors outside social institutions (such as family child-rearing practices). Thus, schools are not only sites where existing power differences come together but they also constitute locations where these power differences are reinforced and reproduced.

In the chapters that follow, the elements of the overview offered in Chapter 1 are further developed. Chapter 2 explores the contemporary empirical research on the relationship between social inequality and the body by examining the two typical ways in which sociology has treated the body, and then advancing a third, post-structuralist, co-constitutive point of view. Chapter 3 examines the theoretical foundations for social class and the body by summarizing the work of Pierre Bourdieu and Annette Lareau, working toward a durable theory of social class in children's bodies in the contexts of home and school. Chapter 4 then takes this theory to the contemporary schooling situation in the United States by asking how some of the significant features of today's school experience might shape children's somatic experience of this compulsory practice. In this chapter, I examine Ruby Payne's *Framework for Understanding Poverty* curriculum for its potential impact on how teachers see working-class and poor children's bodies, and profile the Knowledge is Power Program (KIPP) charter school organization for possible effects on children's bodies. I frame these two examples as part of the larger neoliberal shift influencing schools today, and critique as inhumane the outcomes of an education meant to produce human capital. Contrary to the claims of neoliberal reformers, who view their work as supportive of social justice, I illustrate that these practices are more likely to reinstate common features of social reproduction in schooling by further embedding complex, unexamined corporeal norms into the expectations of school life.

Positioning the author

Lastly, as a researcher and theorist working from a post-structuralist stance relative to the body and social class, I am aware that my own positionality relative to these ideas influences all aspects of this book: the organization, the selection of the relevant data, and the conclusions drawn. As one of my graduate school professors once said, "all scholarship is veiled autobiography," and through writing this book, I have become acutely aware of the truth in this statement. My childhood, like many others, is an interesting alchemy of socioeconomic and social class experiences, one that is hard to characterize in a "pure" category of class assignment. Born and raised in Washington State, my father went to law school on the GI Bill after his time in the military. His experience growing up in decidedly working-class conditions inculcated his serious commitment to social mobility, especially the sort gained through education. My early experiences with him mirrored Lareau's concerted cultivation. Significant to my early childhood were the many, many lessons I took for ballet, piano, horseback riding, ice skating, swimming, tennis and downhill skiing. My father also believed that private school was critical for improving one's life chances. He enrolled my brother and me at The Little School, in Bellevue, Washington, a small experimental elementary school that focused on community building and fostering student confidence in academic and co-curricular realms. I recall significant intellectual freedom at The Little School. It is salient to me now that I received enormous exposure to both cognitive and corporeal aspects of the world. During this period, I learned that the body and the mind were to be worked upon, improved, and instructed.

I took these lessons with me as I began living with my mother and step-father at the age of 15. This part of my upbringing was more middle-class; my mother had a secure position working for the State of Washington and my step-father was in sales. My many lessons ended (with the exception of piano), in part because I was aware of the limited finances for such experiences. My mother led me to think of my body not as feature of myself that needed alteration but as a part of me that just was. I recall feeling that who I was was enough, perhaps for the first time. My life became more typically middle-class by attending public high school and then going on to Washington State University for a major in psychology. I did not apply to any other college; the choice of my state land-grant institution seemed right in a way that was confirmed by my new social class status and the fact that many others from my high school in my working-class/middle-class town were also attending. Only those students who were deemed "upper-class" went to Stanford, Reed, or Whitman. The rest of us went to WSU. I was part of the "rest."

Starting in graduate school and continuing into my professional life, I have developed an awareness for how my social class and socioeconomic positions influence my thinking about and experience of higher education, which has maintained my professional interest in considering questions related to social class. In the multiculturalism course I teach, social class influences are a significant focus. I have written other pieces on the influence of social class on students at my institution (Henry 2005), and in the past three years have begun focusing more intently on the experiences of young children in early classroom life (Henry 2013). My graduate school education in social foundations of education, with a concentration in sociology of education, informs the critical, theoretical lens I take on schooling. Early in my program at the University of Virginia, the seminal question of how schools could claim to confer equal opportunity yet actually construct its ontological opposite intrigued me. As such, I aim my professional work to examine the mechanisms through which schools work "to illuminate the ways in which educational policy and practice are connected to the relations of exploitation and domination in the larger society" (Apple, quoted in Au 2009: 18). My work here brings together these colliding interests about the power of schooling and the influence of social class, focusing on the body and embodiment as a new location from which to see classroom life in order to unravel systems of social reproduction in schools.

Notes

1 All names are pseudonyms to protect the identity of children and school personnel.
2 Readers interested in gender identity and the body would be well advised to consult work from (Butler 1993 and 2006; Walkerdine 1990); race (Hobson 2012; Holloway 2011; Skeggs 2004 and 2005), (dis)ability (Davis 1995; Thomson 1996), and the many other references used in this text.
3 There is a developing line of theory in education and psychology emphasizing the importance of "grit, curiosity, and character" over sheer cognitive capacity (see Tough 2012; Almlund et al. 2011; Duckworth and Seligman 2005; Heckman 1999). This literature targets the development of capacities seen to be constitutive of self-discipline and self-control and will be explored in greater depth in Chapter 3 when examining the impact of neoliberal educational agendas on curriculum and schools.

2
Social Class Inequities and the Body

Abstract: *This chapter familiarizes readers with the empirical landscape surrounding the study of social class and the body. Three orientations to this research are explored: two bidirectional orientations (1) different kinds of bodies experience different types of stratification and (2) social stratification constructs certain bodily outcomes, and a third, co-constitutive point of view (bodies and stratifying practices mutually influence one another). This chapter reviews research on adults and then summarizes recent findings relative to children in all three empirical orientations. It concludes by arguing that the co-constitutive point of view is the most promising for elucidating the relationship between social class and children's bodies, due to its focus on children's agentic capacities.*

Keywords: bodily outcomes; children's agency; stratification

Henry, Sue Ellen. *Children's Bodies in Schools: Corporeal Performances of Social Class.* New York, Palgrave Macmillan, 2014. DOI: 10.1057/9781137442635.0005.

This chapter familiarizes readers with the empirical landscape surrounding the study of social class and the body. In this literature, three orientations to the relationship between social class and the body are prominent. The first bidirectional approach focuses on social outcomes associated with bodies that do not fit easily within society norms; the second bidirectional approach emphasizes the influence of class inequality on bodily outcomes; and the third approach seeks to characterize the co-constitutive nature of bodies and their social milieu (Mason 2013).

The first bidirectional approach maintains that individuals with particular kinds of bodies experience different types of social stratification, leading to class inequality. Examples of this position are the copious data documenting labor market discrimination against people of nonnormative size and the types of stigma that overweight children face in school. The second bidirectional approach maintains that class inequality causes certain bodily outcomes. Studies representative of this point of view often consider the impact of low-income status on physical and mental health. The third more complex and interactive, post-structuralist orientation has yet to be fully explored relative to social class, but developments in the study of gender, race, and (dis)ability identity provide promising new insights. Considering the body from this more interactive orientation illustrates the ways in which bodies and social stratifying practices in institutions such as schools are *co-constitutive* (Mason 2013). By co-constitutive, I mean that bodies and the institutionally framed social structures they encounter work in an intersectional manner to reinforce and contradict each other. Bodies influence social contexts, and social contexts influence bodies.

This intersectional approach is adopted by researchers working from a post-structuralist stance, and has been utilized primarily by theorists in Gender Studies (Butler 2006), Disability Studies (Davis 1995; Davis and Bérubé 2002; Holt 2004), and Fat Studies (Farrell 2011; Rothblum and Solovay 2009). These researchers and theorists attempt to uncover the complexity inherent in understanding the ways bodies work in social situations and the ways social contexts work on bodies. As Mason (2013) asserts, "in heeding the body's insistent materiality—not just its usefulness as a symbol or as a container for the mind—we must grapple with the ways that the physical body gives off a wide range of meanings, some of which appear contradictory or work in combination to constitute the whole person" (694). This intersectional view has the benefit of seeing individuals as agentic forces and allows the social context to be understood as a multidimensional, dynamic space, providing greater insight into the complexity of social change. Such a position is particularly novel when examining the experiences of children, a population whose agentic power is typically left unexamined and overlooked.

Implicit in all three of these positions relative to social class and the body are assertions about self-control. Self-control comes to the fore because it is a primary mechanism through which bodily differences lead to bodily inequality (Mason 2013). For example, the common thinking goes that people of nonnormative size could, if they were to practice self-control and self-discipline, change their bodies to be more fitting to social norms. The same thinking is commonly applied to other forms of bodily difference, such as gestural distinctions and vocal distinctions. The idea that self-control is the central element necessary to transform the body has a deep history in science and draws from the deeply racist origins of early scientific and psychological thought that attempted to ascertain various psychological dispositions that correlated with certain races. This idea also has particular purchase in a capitalist society where one's value is related to one's economic productivity. Any feature that apparently differentiates one from the "norm" diminishes one's stature. Importantly, however, this story of self-control is not a coherent one. Early evolutionary science sought to establish self-control as an outgrowth of bodily characteristics of white men, an ascribed quality rather than an achieved one. However, as we will see, even seeing self-control as an "achieved" status does not inoculate such thinking from working as a source for negative stigma against people of corporeal distinction.

This chapter explores these research trajectories, starting with a review of those studies that document the way bodily differences create social inequity. Such studies are important because they illustrate the stratification outcomes of bodily difference, and how those outcomes become enduring forms of (bodily) inequality. It then shifts to explore the contemporary research from the opposite perspective, focusing on the way social class differences creates bodily differences. Studies from this point of view are important because they highlight the corporeal consequences of life in different social class strata. In both of these sections, I begin by summarizing some of the most recent literature on the experience of adults, which is more prevalent. I then shift to a focus on children and draw out the consistent features that exist between these two populations.

Bodily influences on social class

Researchers studying bodily influence on class focus on the ways particular kinds of bodies, and the cultural meanings ascribed to them, contribute to social stratification. Much research in this area documents the kinds of unearned advantages and disadvantages that individuals with varying bodily features experience in social institutions. This work focuses on the benefits and penalties that individuals with both normative and nonnormative bodies experience, and then considers the social class implications of such treatment. One central emphasis in this orientation is the dynamics of body size in the labor market. In what follows, I summarize the literature on the experiences of adults and children with nonnormative body size, specifically the influence of obesity and overweight status on lived experience.

Adult experiences

In the adult realm, studies of discrimination against job candidates and employees with nonnormative bodies serve as important examples of how bodily difference shapes class experience. Mason (2013) describes this work as a "mounting pile" of academic evidence that documents these trends in the labor market (Cawley 2004; Conley and Glauber 2005; Puhl and Heuer 2009). Consistent data show, for example, that overweight adults are stereotyped negatively throughout society (Crocker, Cornwell, and Major 1993), degraded by both strangers and intimates (Crandall 1994), and report other forms of discrimination at higher rates than their "normal" weight counterparts (Carr and Friedman 2005). These patterns serve as the foundation for discrimination that occurs in the workplace, which seems more directed at jobseekers in white-collar professions (Carr and Friedman 2005), white job candidates as opposed to black and Hispanic applicants, and women more than men (Conley and Glauber, 2007).

In fact, being overweight for women seems to have enduring effects, not only for employment status but also for other factors associated with social class status. Conley and Glauber (2007) found that overweight status was associated with a 18% reduction in women's wages, a 25% reduction in women's family income, and a 16% reduction in a women's probability of marriage. Recent research suggests that these outcomes are far more robust and persistent than originally thought (Conley and

Glauber 2005). Some studies suggest that when overweight women do marry, their husbands earn lower than average incomes compared to those of slender women (Averett and Korenman 1996). According to this research, 50–95 percent of overweight women's lower economic status is explained by the differences in marriage probabilities and spouse's lower earnings. To a considerable degree, pervasive negative stereotypes of nonnormative bodies explain these trends. Overweight people are routinely ascribed personality characteristics such as laziness, selfishness, and emotional impairment (Pingitore, Dugoni, Scott, and Spring 1994). Couple these trends with gender discrimination, and a toxic alchemy ensues.

Beyond the powerful effects of these trends on individuals' lives, another component that makes them damaging is the internalization of these beliefs by large-bodied individuals (Carels et al. 2009). One study (Demuth, Czerniak, and Ziółkowska-Łajp 2013) found that women were particularly vulnerable to internalizing social views of overweight status. In this study, women who self-assessed themselves as overweight had the greatest body mass index (BMI) and were the most dissatisfied with their body image. Women who believed that their body weight corresponded to expected norms had average satisfaction with their bodies, and those women most satisfied with their bodies had normal BMI values. This research supports the idea that individuals, particularly women, can develop skewed thinking about their own bodies when confronted with powerful social messages about what normative bodies look like. Such thinking is consistent with sociologist Charles Cooley's notion of the Looking Glass Self, which asserts that individuals' self-perceptions are not solely of their own making, but are mediated through the feedback they receive about themselves from the social world (Cooley 1992). In what follows, we will see that the messages that overweight children receive about themselves in the world of school comprise a subtle yet consistent set of negative ideas, emerging from the notion that overweight status is a sign of lacking self-control.

Children's experiences

In the realm of children, this story unfolds in a manner similar to that of adults, particularly for the problem of childhood obesity. While there has been some leveling off from the rapid rise in obesity documented in the 1980s and 1990s, obesity rates for children remain an area of significant concern (Ogden, Carroll, Kit, and Flegal 2012). In 2012, the Centers for Disease Control reported that 16.9% of children and adolescents in the United States were obese and that this overall rate remained steady with earlier data collected in 2007–2008 (Ogden et al. 2012). A recent Harvard School of Public Health publication indicates that certain populations have a much higher risk for obesity, namely boys, and both Hispanic and non-Hispanic blacks. Other research suggests that girls who become overweight in the first four years of their school experience are more likely to experience diminished academic performance (Datar and Sturm 2006). Such situations increase the likelihood that overweight children will be stigmatized and discriminated against, and the research bears out that these are typical experiences for obese children.

The mounting literature on weight-based ostracism and bullying of overweight and obese children suggests that schools are a prime location for weight-based discrimination against young people ("Report on Discrimination due to Physical Size" 1994). To address this concern, the National Education Association distributed a report in 1994 calling for greater attention to size discrimination among school-age children. What is perhaps surprising about the need for such educational efforts is that despite being deeply committed to child welfare and development, teachers and school staff remain susceptible to stereotypes about obesity.

Dietz's (1998) review of the literature on the schooling experiences of obese and overweight children found that the discrimination they experience is largely institutionalized and based upon unrealistic expectations associated with teachers' inaccurate interpretations of overweight children's bodies. Because overweight children are often taller than their age-graded peers, educators who do not know the age of overweight children may assume them to be more mature and hold different corporeal and cognitive expectations for them. One mechanism for this institutionalization of discrimination is teachers' lack of awareness of the stereotypes they hold of overweight individuals. O'Brien, Hunter, and Banks (2007) found that physical education teachers in training in New Zealand held "strong negative prejudice" against overweight individuals, at rates significantly greater than a control group. Similar evidence of prejudice and its consequences is found throughout the literature, supporting the idea that overweight children are seen by educators and other school personnel as "less tidy, more emotional, less likely to succeed at work" and coming from families experiencing problems (Neumark-Sztainer, Story, and Harris

1999). Similarly disturbing results were found by Greenleaf and Weiller (2005), whose study of physical education teachers indicated higher reported expectations for "normal-weight" students versus overweight students on a range of corporeal performance capacities. Demonstrating the difficulty of escaping the ubiquitous, negative social beliefs attributed to overweight individuals, participants in this study also indicated moderate support of anti-fat attitudes, while agreeing with the sentiment that childhood obesity is a significant concern and that schools are not doing enough to interrupt such patterns among the school-age population.

Other studies on childhood obesity find similar trends among educators. Neumark-Sztainer, Story, and Harris (1999) found that 28% of teachers they surveyed indicated that "becoming obese is one of the worst things that could happen to a person" (6). In a qualitative study of 8th graders, Bauer, Yang, and Austin (2004) found that negative comments from school staff members about students' athletic abilities were a contributing factor to self-consciousness among students and were associated with a reduction in children's participation during recess and physical education classes.

Surprisingly, these experiences do not seem to influence academic achievement among overweight youth. Zavodny (2013) conducted a longitudinal study of K-8th grade children, sampling standardized test scores in reading, math, and science and teacher assessments at five intervals across nine years. Her findings indicate that a child's weight is not generally related to his/her academic achievement in these subject areas, but is significantly negatively related to teachers' assessment of children's ability in reading and math. Zavodny's (2013) work confirms other research that while overweight children experience higher incidences of bullying (Rothblum and Solovay 2009; Storch et al. 2007), negative influences on quality of life (Friedlander SL et al. 2003), and lower self-esteem (among Hispanic and non-Hispanic white girls) (Strauss 2000), these experiences do not seem to impact students' performance on standardized tests (Caird et al. 2013; Kaestner and Grossman 2009). Caird et al.'s (2013) review of the literature on the association between weight and academic achievement suggests that weight alone appears to explain very little of the variation in academic achievement among young learners; other factors, such as school-level features (e.g., funding, urban status, class size) and ethnic diversity of the school population, were stronger variables in explaining achievement scores.

While the data suggest that overweight status in children is not an indicator of their potential academic performance, commonly held beliefs about the correspondence between certain bodily presentations and cognitive and personality traits remain a persistent notion, even among educators. Given this inconsistency, what accounts for these enduring beliefs among teachers? I take up this question by exploring the biological determinism that serves as an underpinning for negative stereotyping of nonnormative individuals. Establishing the link between biological determinism and negative stereotypes is fundamental to fully understand the ways in which self-control operates as a mechanism for converting bodily differences into bodily inequalities.

Faulty biological origins for stereotypical thinking

Beliefs about the parity between particular body types and personality dispositions have at their epicenter the notion that there is a biological basis for traits such as laziness. While discredited by significant research in the natural and social sciences, this view has historically been a dominant force in the study of race and racism and still has popular support among the public with regard to weight and bodily presentation. As Mason (2013) asserts, "one of the most persistent beliefs about bodily difference comes to us in the form of racial difference" (687). The embodiment of racial differences was seen by early scientists (and by some people still today) as indicative of biologically distinct races that carried with them distinct psychological, cognitive, and moral differences. As Stitzlein (2008) affirms, "[r]ace was—and frequently still is—a classification system based on physical characteristics of the body that can be used to describe and make predictions about human groups" (31–32). Biological science now confirms the lack of correspondence between biological differences such as melanin in skin and human variation in cognitive capacities such as intelligence, but the presumption of biological determinism that informed much early science in biology, psychology, and anthropology remains pervasive in the general public. Contemporary examples of this line of thinking are easily seen in Richard Herrnstein and Charles Murray's (1996) book *The Bell Curve*, which sought to scientifically confirm the argument that intellectual differences are rooted in biological racial differences.

First advanced by Arthur Jensen in 1969 (1969; 1973), theories about the racial basis of intelligence have now largely been dismissed in academic circles. Yet the orientation persists in some disciplines, such as medical research focused on the development of race-specific pharmaceuticals. While controversial, in 2005 the Food and Drug Administration approved the use of BiDil, a drug used to treat heart failure for African Americans alone (Brody and Hunt 2006; Inda 2013; Sankar 2005). Critics maintain that such practices reify commonly held notions that African American bodies are biologically different from the bodies of other races, which then leads to assumptions and prescriptive ideas about differences in personality and disposition emerging from these biological distinctions.

Following this line of thinking, researchers have hypothesized that allegiance to the Protestant Work Ethic may be a contributing factor to the negative attributions educators, employers, peers, and even parents hold about overweight individuals. From this perspective, weight loss or gain is an individual-level phenomenon, simply requiring "self-control" (Musher-Eizenman et al. 2004; Neumark-Sztainer, Story, and Harris 1999). The notion that a lack of self-control in some individuals results in their becoming overweight offers a "common sense" rationale for some to hold negative beliefs about others. Similar to the "reasoned" discrimination that results from (incorrectly) viewing race and gender as predetermined, biologically based categories, viewing nonnormative bodies as having differences that are fixed and unchanging over time is equally harmful.

There are, however, some important differences in how race, gender, and class are typically conceived. Race and gender are commonly presumed to be more fixed than variable (although research has persuasively argued that it is more accurate to understand these terms as less categorical and more fluid). Social class in the US context, on the other hand, like body weight, is generally perceived by the public as a category of choice. Consequently, essentialist biological views held by the general public tend to be connected more to race and gender, and less to social class, due to the presumption of malleability. And yet, these differences notwithstanding, the notion of self-control is still linked with dominant conceptions related to race, gender, and social class. For race and gender, the assumption of rigidity gives rise to the idea that personality characteristics, such as laziness and wildness for African Americans and emotionality for women, are both natural and fixed. This perspective on race and gender suggests that self-control is an essential element necessary to counteract their "natural" personality tendencies. With regard to social class, the idea is that sufficient self-discipline and control allows one's social class status to be altered. Furthermore, such a position suggests that those who are able to alter their social class status are morally stronger. Thus, while the idea of self-control is a flexible one, it remains a critical fulcrum on which bodily difference becomes legitimized inequality.

In the next section, I explore the other common research orientation in studies on the body: the ways in which class shapes bodily comportment and corporeal performance. A similar belief about the centrality of self-control underlies this work, albeit from a slightly different angle. In this point of view, social class is understood as a force that either maintains self-control or perpetuates enduring problems in managing self-control. While not the intention of researchers, stigmatizing beliefs such as the "culture of poverty" argument have emerged from this research.

Social class influences on the body

We in the United States hold some very pervasive and persistent beliefs about social class, most of which conflict with reality (Sackrey, Schneider and Knoedler 2010). There is a widely held myth that social class is highly mutable and that schooling is a significant contributor to the mobility that students will experience in their lifetime. As Barber (1994) suggests, we have a enduring belief that ours is a class-neutral society, an "aristocracy of everyone." As a class-neutral society, our ability to talk about social class is severely limited. And yet, even under these illusions, social science generates copious data suggesting that there are profound consequences for the body based upon social class position, both for adults and children (Mason, 2013).

Adult experiences

Bucking the widespread trend to avoid discussion of social class in public media, Scott's (2005) five-part series in *The New York Times* asserts that there is a significant positive correlation between social class status and physical health. Having the material resources to access preventive health care and biomedical innovation for the treatment of disease are two elements that most profoundly influence classed bodies. Indeed, data indicate that upper-middle-class Americans live longer and better than those at the bottom of the social class scale (Navarro 1991). Indeed, Navarro (1991) also finds that class is a stronger predictor of mortality rates among Americans than race.

Lack of access to material resources among those in lower income brackets influences not only health care, but also increases residential segregation (Massey 1996), exposure to high levels of street crime, and other environmental hazards (Williams, McClellan, and Rivlin 2010), all of which contribute to increased stress. According to Mirowski and Ross (1989, cited in Sackrey et al. 2010), increased psychological stress in these situations arises due to the lack of individual control created by these conditions. In short, the lack of control leads to poor health. A 2003 report from the World Health Organization demonstrated that lack of control in one's work life, more than exposure to toxins or an otherwise dangerous work environment, is associated with ill-health.

> Several European workplace studies show that health suffers when people have little opportunity to use their skills and low decision-making authority. Having little control over one's work is particularly strongly related to an increased risk of lower-back pain, sickness absence, and cardiovascular disease. These risks have been found to be independent of the psychological characteristics of the people studied. In short, they seem to be related to the work environment. (cited in Sackrey, Schneider, Knoedler 2010: 148)

Importantly, the lack of control referenced here is quite different from the notion of a lack of self-control. These data make clear that diminished discretion at work, a limited amount of personal authority over one's schedule, determination of duties and the like are the components of work life that have detrimental effects on workers' health. This "lack of control" is distinguished from self-control in that even when individuals in these circumstances have self-control, there are structures in the work environment that thwart its successful application.

Notably, data in this field do not indicate that poor people are the only ones living with stress. Rather, high socioeconomic status individuals, who manage the stress they experience with broad access to preventive health care and medical treatment of disease, are less likely to be overweight, and more likely to exercise greater personal discretion throughout their work day, all of which expand their life expectancy and reduce the likelihood of chronic ill-health.

Children's experiences

As one might expect, similar patterns are seen in children as well. Material differences in children's life experiences dramatically shape their physiological health and their futures (Bradley and Corwyn 2002;

Brooks-Gunn and Duncan 1997). Abundant research documents the profound impact that financial hardship, food insecurity, poor housing, inadequate access to health care, exposure to environmental toxins, and attendance at poorly resourced schools (to name just a few) make on children's health (Wilkinson and Pickett 2006), education (Sacker, Schoon, and Bartley 2002), and overall welfare (Wilkinson 2006). Recent research has concluded that material hardships have a particularly significant influence on childhood mortality, physical health, and cognitive differences (Bradley and Corwyn 2002), even while acknowledging that there is a variety of ways to measure socioeconomic status.

One of the strongest findings from the literature is the relationship between poverty and childhood mortality. In their review of studies of unintended childhood traumas that most commonly lead to childhood mortality, Laflamme, Hasselberg, and Burrows (2010) find that socioeconomic status remains a critical variable related to the five most frequent forms of accidents among children: vehicular accidents, poisoning, burns, drowning, and falls. These researchers posit that social class serves as a "fundamental cause" for the social distribution of resources available that protect children from these unintended harms.

> The fundamental causes theory suggests that a range of resources susceptible to protect one's health and safety are socially distributed, implying that people of higher socioeconomic status hold an advantage in warding off threats to their—and their offspring's—wellbeing. The theory predicts that socioeconomic status is more strongly associated with health outcomes for which prevention and treatment measures are known, which largely applies to unintentional injuries. (Laflamme, Hasselberg, and Burrows 2010: 19)

Although studies following children's health have utilized a variety of measures of social class and socioeconomic status, they have consistently reached similar conclusions.

With regard to physical health, Yoo, Slack, and Holl (2009) found that proximal measures of material difficulty and hardship were important to understand the mutual influence of hardship indicators on children's general health. This approach is more complex than the more common means of measuring material hardship through a single variable, such as housing. In particular, these researchers found that children who were reported by their caregivers to be living in poor-quality housing and experiencing frequent food hardship were less likely to be in excellent health than were children living in better conditions. The same was true of children whose caregivers reported financial difficulties in meeting medical needs. These effects remained even when researchers controlled for other hardship variables, suggesting that financial difficulties, food hardship, and poor-quality housing are particularly salient when predicting health outcomes for low-income children.

After parents, school personnel are often some of the first in the community to recognize the effects of material hardship on children; educators are particularly concerned with the effects of poverty on cognitive development. Copious research documents the long-term effects of various physiological experiences associated with poverty on neurological development, namely insufficient cognitive stimulation, stunting, iodine deficiency, and iron-deficiency anemia (Walker et al. 2011). Recent research has focused on the particular neural mechanisms through which such effects take place in the brain. Studies such as these differ from epidemiological or sociological approaches in that they attempt to codify the physiological systems that serve as the basis for cognitive and affective neurological structures, which researchers in this field claim are influenced by socioeconomic status.

In their quest to verify the neurological mechanisms most influenced by particular environmental stimuli, Hackman, Farah, and Meaney (2010) maintain that neuroscience in humans and animals "has provided candidate mechanisms for the cause-effect relationships between socioeconomic status and neural development" (651). Their research finds that some of these relationships are reversible, and they suggest that such research can shape policies to "prevent and remediate" the neural effects of low childhood socioeconomic status (651), which they maintain is a form of "social causation" of social selection (653). One possible pathway of the effects of childhood poverty is the creation of chronic stress during early developmental years (Tough 2012). Recent neurological research involving fMRIs in 49 participants in a longitudinal design finds that chronic childhood stress associated with poverty (measured in family income) was a significant predictor of reduced emotional regulation in participants in adulthood (Kim et al. 2013). Senior author of the study, Dr. K. Luan Phan, maintains that "our findings suggest that the stress-burden of growing up poor may be an underlying mechanism that accounts for the relationship between poverty as a child and how well your brain works as an adult" (Mcginnis Gonzalez 2013).

The corporeal consequences of these early social class effects become more evident as children enter school. Utilizing the US Department of Education's Early Childhood Longitudinal Study (ECLS), Lee and Burkham (2002) maintain that important differences in achievement scores in mathematics and early literacy are frequently observed in children of different social class status (Lee and Burkam 2002). Their study demonstrates that social class mediates some early childhood experiences that are highly correlated to cognitive gains (and lack of gains), such as access to quality child care, home reading practices, home computer use, and television use habits. These researchers explain that even after accounting for racial and ethnic differences, cognitive differences continue to vary by social class status. In fact, social class and its correlated practices account for the "unique variation" in cognitive scores among children of difference social class backgrounds (Lee and Burkam 2002).

Another study illustrating cognitive difference resulting from social class background comes from Stipek and Ryan (1997). These researchers' analysis of cognitive competencies and motivation in a subsample of 88 preschool and kindergarten children (N=233) revealed significantly poorer performance among children of low-income status compared to economically advantaged children. In this sample, even after accounting for children who had attended at least one year of preschool, a large socioeconomic gap was found for children on all measures of cognitive competency (word knowledge, counting/sorting, number memory/math achievement/puzzle solving, conceptual grouping, verbal fluency, reading achievement). The researchers maintain that the gap can be practically understood as about one year of development: "for some of the cognitive measures...the disadvantaged kindergarteners had lower scores than advantaged preschoolers had at the beginning of the year, suggesting at least a year's delay" (Stipek and Ryan 1997: 720).

Interestingly, differences in motivation for school, attitude toward school and expectations for school success *did not* vary according to social class status (Stipek and Ryan 1997). Such a finding counters the all too common notion that poor parents' low support of education fosters children who also do not care about school. While research has found an important link between internal motivation for education and school achievement among older children (Stipek 1993; Stipek and Gralinski 1996), such differences are not common among children in the primary grades.

Stipek and Ryan's (1997) work demonstrates the ways in which social class influences children's ability on typical school-based knowledge and tasks. These researchers acknowledge that there are cognitive tasks that socioeconomically disadvantaged children might perform better than their advantaged counterparts, such as "practice knowledge or social problem solving" (Stipek and Ryan 1997: 720). This comment exemplifies that school practice is not a set of neutral tasks that are universally experienced by children in all homes in the United States. Rather, school practices represent a set of experiences that are profoundly influenced by the social class position of children who enact them, instructional designers who write the curriculum, and teachers who impart the curriculum, namely middle- and upper-middle-class, educated members of society. Inherent in this complex world of school are embedded, largely tacit expectations about the body that some children come to school already familiar with, and corporeal practices that other children are still learning. Just as "school readiness" capacities are not class-neutral, neither are the expectations for self-control that motivate the corporeal requirements of contemporary elementary schooling.

The complexity of schooling and the tensions between the multiple agentic forces in schools (adults and children) sets the foundation for why a co-constitutive orientation to understanding bodies in social settings is so important. Before moving to an examination of the current literature in the co-constitutive realm, I first summarize some of the benefits and limitations of the two perspectives on the relationship between bodies and social contexts presented thus far. There are significant accomplishments noted here in the abundant research from these orientations; there are also serious limitations that the co-constitutive point of view can address.

Bodies → social class/social class → bodies: benefits, limitations, and implications for self-control

There is no denying that material differences make a difference in the quality of life that children experience. The big picture outcomes are obvious: poverty creates bodies at risk and bodies at risk are frequently interpreted in certain negative ways in social institutions that reify their at-risk status. Studies from both of the causal directions explored in the previous sections offer educators, researchers, and politicians firm ground from which to argue for equalizing material resources. Because these studies often use powerful datasets such as the NELS-88 and the Panel Study of Income Dynamics, their findings are generalizable. Important school-related policy can result from these findings if educators learn that students with certain types of bodies are experiencing school in negative ways; studies such as these have the potential to help educators consider the consequences of various school policies on the bodies of children in their care. Indeed, this expansive literature base has exposed the significant correlations between negative stereotypes of people with nonnormative bodies and the consequences they face in social institutions, as well as illustrated the effects of social class on the physical and mental health of the body. With almost half of all American public school students living in poverty (Sparks 2013), it is essential for educators to understand the relationships between poverty and other social conditions such as health, residential segregation, crime, neurological development, and school achievement.

There are, however, critical issues that must be taken up with the research that results from these two orientations, the first of which is that interpreting this research requires a deep commitment to considering people in their wholeness and to avoid essentializing them based upon the bodies they possess or the ways in which social institutions shape their bodies. Research focused on children's bodies coupled with widely held notions of a biological basis for personality and moral attitudes risks reinforcing dominant stereotypes. While certainly most researchers working from these points of view do not intend to support genetic determinism, research resulting from these views can be used to categorize people in narrow ways. Activities in the biologically determined intelligence movement, such as Lewis' culture of poverty argument and Herrnstein and Murray's more recent iteration, are examples. As we will see in Chapter 4, some contemporary programs focused on teaching poor children also serve as examples of the nefarious effects of the inappropriate use of data emerging from these camps.

Even if researchers were very careful (as most are) not to essentialize children based upon a particular quality of their body (such as weight), a remaining significant concern is that this research begins with a version of the "normative" body through its contrasting examination of "non-normative" bodies. The lack of a critical lens placed on what is "normative" reinforces the idea that if all bodies could approximate the norm, then social inequality would eventually disappear. Movements such as Healthy at any Size, and disciplinary studies such as Fat Studies and Disability Studies, attempt to decouple the linkage between body appearance and psychological factors such as tidiness and determination. These theoretical approaches are also working to reduce the stigmatized cultural meanings associated with particular bodies. For example, in (Dis)ability studies, scholars question the conceptions of "health" as an "unmarked, often-invisible norm against which people with disabilities, the elderly, and other groups are unfavorably compared" (Mason 2013: 694).

Education-based research which questions "normal" and "appropriate" body practices including eye contact, smile, body posture, and hand position when holding writing instruments, exists and has been around for some time. For example, as early as 1939, educator Luella Cole encouraged teachers not to see a left-handed child as disabled (Cole 1939). As Cole (1939) reminds, an emotional adjustment on the part of the teacher is essential to this reimaging of the left-handed student. "From the first day in school, the left handed child is subject to pressure. Both parents and teachers bewail his condition....Even though nothing is said to him on this point, he may insist on trying to be right-handed because he is uncomfortable under the emotional pressure that he is queer" (Cole 1939). Continuing in this vein, in the last 20 years, well-known researcher Dorothy Bishop has produced significant evidence supporting the lack of relationship between handedness and the prevalence of certain developmental disorders. She asserts that assumptions about the relationship between handedness and developmental problems result from poor research and suspect publishing practices aimed at circulating research with significant results rather than results supporting the null hypothesis. This sort of questioning serves as an example of the kind of critical inquiry necessary to develop understandings of matters that appear settled and therefore mask the political orientation of the research.

From a sociological point of view, each of the causal orientations discussed runs the risk of overstating the effects of structure on the body (both the structure of social class and the structure of certain types of bodies) and underdeveloping the agency of actors in social circumstances. This tension is described as the "structure-agency divide" in sociology, and has a long history in the discipline. Shilling (1997) maintains that this enduring bifurcation results from "the inseparability of society from human activity, the existence of social chance, and the development of individual change" (Shilling 1997: 739). The potential to frame structures that are overdetermined and therefore incapacitating to individual agency is a particular concern for research directed toward children, a population which has often been seen from adult-centric positions that limit children's capacity to act in creative ways (Ausdale and Feagin 2001). Shilling (1997) maintains that the lack of attention to embodied forms of agency truncates work in contemporary sociology even further by overemphasizing "cognitive thought and reflexivity as mediators of agency and structure" and underemphasizing "the somatic mediation" of these factors (Shilling 1997: 737). Shilling (1997) continues by arguing that "[as long as] the body remains irreducible to both society and to nature...it will remain necessary for sociologists to examine how the embodied actor is both partly shaped by society, yet also able to influence its future development" (747).

One particularly important application of the tension between structure and agency inherent in studies of the body arises when considering self-control. Self-control, as discussed earlier, suggests a practice of agency within certain structures, and an acknowledgment by the agent of the structures that influence one's agency. Self-control cannot mean sheer compliance or obedience; if it did, the control would be exclusively external rather than internal. Instead, self-control happens in contexts that have both (1) structures that influence the possibilities for agency that one experiences and (2) structures that are themselves influenced by the forms of agency practiced by agents in those social spaces.

Education is critical for cultivating individuals who can operate as social agents by creating classrooms that require students to develop and practice these capacities. As philosopher John Dewey reminds us, "the ideal aim of education is creation of the power of self-control" (Dewey 2007). Later, in *The Public and its Problems* (1927), Dewey explains the importance of self-governance, suggesting that civic participation requires self-direction such that individuals are capable of seeing beyond their own limited interests toward those interests they share with others. Dewey advocated that individuals develop self-control while participating in the regular negotiation of shared boundaries, a process he termed "democracy." Well-known Dewey biographer Robert Westbrook writes of Dewey's philosophy that,

> Democracy was the form of associated life which provided the opportunity for the full flowering of individuality, and the "keynote of democracy" was "the necessity for the participation of every mature human being in the formation of the values that regulate the living of men together." (Westbrook 1991: 433)

Because associated life was essential for the development of individuality, "the individual must have the opportunity to participate in the direction of his life" (Westbrook 1991: 433). For Dewey, school served as a central field for the development of these faculties in children.

Applied to the context of schools, the question of how the body is implicated in navigating this narrow channel between all-consuming structure and complete individual agency is taken up by Carrie Noland in her 2010 book *Agency and Embodiment: Performing Gestures/Producing Culture*. In articulating the actions of the body, Noland prefers the term "gesture" over "movement," as gesture more strongly focuses on "the *specific* moving body inevitably inflecting acquired gestural routines and instantiating them in a revised form" that exemplifies the agency of the performer (Noland 2010: 7, italics in original). For Noland, gesture works as "organized forms of kinesis through which subjects navigate and alter their worlds" (Noland 2010: 4) and is deeply shaped by culture and structures that arise from culture. Such an account of gesture incorporates agency because, as Noland holds, "if moving bodies perform in innovative ways, it is not because they manage to move without acquired gestural routines but because they gain knowledge *as a result of performing them*" (Noland 2010: 7). Thus, the routines of home- and school-based corporeal performances offer children an insight into the agentic opportunities that exist within the performances they grow accustomed to, such as lining up, moving from one part of the room to another, preparing for direct instruction, etc. By accounting for routine habitual movement that gives rise to gesture (bodily technique infused with agentic qualities), Noland (2010) illuminates how we might attempt to view the body intersectionally, indicating both the structural contexts within which the body exists and the agentic possibilities of one's body. Noland (2010) reminds us that agency can mean resistance, surely, but it can also signify, as Tim Ingold has claimed, "the discovery of the individual body's singular 'capacities of awareness and response'" (Noland 2010: 7). This is a reconception of self-control suggesting that an accounting of children's bodies is possible and necessary.

While very little research exists in the sociology of the body relative to children's bodies and social class, there is growing set of studies focusing on children and the school-based co-creation of racial and (dis)ability identities that includes deliberate attention to the workings of the body. This contextualized subjectivity is the focus of studies framed by the co-constitutive point of view. As we will see in the next section, these studies attempt to draw a picture of agents' bodies in social settings quite different from the work outlined in the previous two orientations. By incorporating actors' agentic capacities into the research field, the pathways through which bodies shape social contexts and social contexts shape bodies are illuminated.

Co-constitutive constructions of children's bodies and social class

Before hypothesizing about the relationship between children's bodies and social class in contemporary school settings, I wish to explore literature on the co-constitutive nature of race, gender, and (dis)ability to mine it for the implications that arise for the study of social class. As Mason (2013) contends, Gender, Race and (Dis)ability Studies provide useful templates for the study of co-constitutive conceptions of social class and the body. In particular, two interconnected ideas regarding children and their bodies emerge from this literature: (1) the importance of looking for the inherent agentic qualities of children's actions, particularly corporeal performances of their agency and (2) the ways in which corporeal actions manifest in the various identities children explore. Additionally, because this literature attempts to record and analyze the interactional features of an identity marker (such as (dis)ability) and corresponding corporeal and verbal consequences, researchers working from a post-structuralist point of view more often utilize detailed, qualitative methodologies. Though a detailed analysis of social class with respect to children's bodies has not yet emerged, these fields of study offer foundational insights that are critical to the study of social class and its embodiment in children.

Children's agency

Central to a co-constitutive perspective is seeing children in a very different light than is traditional to the study of children's development. Rather than seeing children as apprenticing, diminutive adults, or "innocent" of adult foibles (such as racism), this literature sees children as conscious, determined actors in and on their social world. As such, this literature and the theoretical frameworks behind it, while diverse in nature, agree on questioning traditional developmental theory that dismisses children's agentic capacities (Skattebol 2006). Such post-structural analysis takes as its starting point the notion that "children draw on dominant discourses to establish social power" (Skattebol 2006: 508). As Holt (2004) contends, researchers working from post-structuralist, co-constitutive points of view attempt to reframe children from "objects of socialisation" to "critical social agents" (Holt 2004).

Such an orienting principle gives rise to the consistent emphasis in this literature on the role of agency and seeing children as agentic forces in school settings. Several examples of this idea can be seen in Skattebol's (2006) research in a preschool/day-care setting in Australia. Her study examines the ways in which young children (four- to five-year-olds) use their bodies to assert various identities, particularly those of gender and age-related importance. Skattebol's view of children as legitimate agentic forces in the preschool leads her to observe the children's verbal and nonverbal actions closely, and to see these performances as attempts to influence people and the social setting. One boy who was new to the center in the year of the research offered Skattebol significant insights into the importance of being a boy. Soon after Kyle arrived at the school, he began to try to subvert the center's conscious philosophy of gender-neutral play, coupling his assertion of the appropriateness of masculine play with the powerful motivator for being "older." As Skattebol (2006) recounts, Kyle worked hard to develop a particular friendship with Zac, a longtime member of the school community, with his new approach:

> During the early stages of this friendship, Kyle made sustained attempts to establish an affiliation through male exclusivity. He would try to interest Zac in playing with trucks and trains, but rejected any girls who attempted to join.... One afternoon Kyle came outside to join the play. Zac was catching his breath during a chase scene in a monster catching game. Two girls were taunting Zac from high up in a tree, Zac tried to get Kyle to help him catch the girls. Their interaction was as follows:

ZAC: Let's get 'em.
KYLE: Well, I don't play with girls Zac.
ZAC: I do.
KYLE: Boys don't play with girls.
ZAC: [Looks quizzically.] I do.
KYLE: In my family we don't play with girls.
ZAC: Mine do.
KYLE: Well, we are Indian and we just play with boys.... You want to just play with me?
ZAC: I do play...

KYLE: You just want to play with me?
ZAC: Ummm...over there...we need to get them...[They look at the other children for a while.]
KYLE: Well I am four you know.
ZAC: I'm four too [emphatically].
KYLE: I've got big brothers.
ZAC: Me too. Shane and Danno.
KYLE: My big brothers and I, we just play with boys.
ZAC: My brothers are big.
KYLE: Actually I just play with big boys.
ZAC: I just play with boys too (505–516).

In this extended interaction, Zac is eventually worn down and according to Skattebol (2006), brought around in part by the reference to "big boys,"—that is, boys who are older. In seeing Kyle as a social agent, using socially powerful categories to create the aims he sought, Skattebol (2006) notes "Kyle did not need to do anything to create a desire for big brothers. Zac already possessed this desire. All Kyle had to do to form a friend, it seems, was to associate himself with this desire" (Skattebol 2006: 516).

While this interaction was largely verbal, a later incident emphasizes agency and the use of the body. With their mutual interest in being big and having big brothers, Skattebol notes that both Kyle and Zac "literally 'hung out'" (Skattebol 2006: 518). During free playtimes, both boys would arrange themselves on play equipment and lounge with their bodies in full repose. When a former friend of Zac, Pravit, was not welcomed to join them one day, staff member Susan intervened.

SUSAN: So Kyle who do you want to play?
KYLE: I just want Zac....
SUSAN: Zac, what about you?
ZAC: I want to play boys.
KYLE: I just play with boys.
SUSAN: Pravit?
PRAVIT: I want to play too.
SUSAN: With everyone Pravit?
KYLE: You see Zac and I've got a game here and we just want to play we don't want to play with anyone else.
SUSAN: What game is it?
KYLE: Oh it's a magic game and we can't tell or it'll invisible and then we can't find it.

ZAC: Yep pop! It's gone. [Pravit leaves group.]
SUSAN: What about Pravit, Zac, you always used to play with him and now his feelings are hurt.
KYLE: You see, Susan, now we're not playing at all, we're not doing anything just here boring, boring, boring... you see just like this... *[gazes off into space]*.
SUSAN: Well, I'm sure Pravit could be boring too if he practised. Why don't you teach him how and he can be boring with you.

> With this comment, they turned their gaze from Susan to each other, both shuffled, leaned further back into the [play structure] and gazed into the distance.... [The message] was very clear to me, as an observer, that they were "being" big boys, too old to play. This message was communicated through their citations of teenage bodies with lots of lounging, stretching and haute or low levels of expression and activity. (518–519)

This is a complex, though typical, situation in the early childcare center. Staff would commonly see this situation as an opportunity to help children use verbal negotiation to reach an appropriate solution and to instill the common principle of "being a good friend" by including other children who want to join an activity. Such a position would orient Kyle and Zac's behavior as a classroom management issue rather than a situation in which they are asserting their agency. From this viewpoint, their "agency" comes in the form of resistance to the veiled command of the teacher to incorporate others into their group. But as we can see, one can ask different questions not only about the verbal exchange here but also about the use of Kyle and Zac's bodies to assert a particular point of view, thereby gaining access to a different set of meanings from the interaction. Instead of merely being understood as oppositional, viewing Kyle's actions from the point of view of agency sees him in the throes of learning how to integrate the conceptions of "right play" he has gathered from home with the explicit philosophy of "right play" present in his schooling context. From this view, Kyle's behavior is reframed from a classroom management problem to be solved to one of a learner in the act of growing and developing greater sophistication about how to incorporate himself and his values into social spaces he shares with others.

One important element this interaction reveals is that there is often a link between verbal and corporeal communication (Skattebol 2006). This connection can be both symmetrical and contradictory. Much educational research focuses on linguistic competence and the mastery of formal school language that facilitates social and academic success in school. Focus on children's bodies, however, remains embryonic. Attending to the workings of the body can provide additional information to teachers and researchers on the exchanges taking place. In considering children, Skattebol (2006) maintains that when attending to the body, researchers would be well advised to avoid seeing "children" as a categorical identity. Rather, viewing children's agentic qualities means taking as a given that bodies in motion, bodies that are moving and changing, say something but are also in the process of becoming something else all the time. Indeed, in his practice of his agency, Kyle was in part playing with identity, and asserting his position as a "big boy" by excluding others (girls, Pravit) from the play that they, from his point of view, did not fit.

Trying on identities

From a post-structural, co-constitutive point of view, therefore, it is essential to understand agents' identity(ties) as multiplicative and evolving over time. Holt (2004) illuminates this position by suggesting that a co-constitutive conception of the body requires avoiding traditional and "natural" dualisms. As she notes, bodies are "inscribed within discourses that prioritise differences above multiple similarities" (Holt 2004: 787). One extension of this position is the notion that, contrary to popular adult belief, children aren't always "pretending" to be someone they aren't, but instead are trying on identities in a playful manner to assert some sort of truth about themselves. Skattebol (2006) maintains that there is a realistic quality to the concerted use of the body and voice to declare particular identity moves, such as "becoming school-age" (513). Such moves include "bodily control and manipulation...children would frequently exaggerate their size and posture by arching their backs, pointing their chins upwards and generally puffing out their body mass," even when childrens' actual bodies betrayed a different reality, such as being thin, fine boned, or short in stature (Skattebol 2006: 513). In such situations, students are working their bodies in ways to stress the distinction between how they see themselves (in this case, school-age children, i.e., "big kids") and others in the class whom they classify as "young kids."

A similar strategy for establishing an identity is "othering," asserting an identity for the self by distinguishing oneself from someone else in the social field. Van Ausdale and Feagin's (2001) study of a childcare center offers interesting insights into how children use race and racism, both verbally and corporeally, to assert a racial identity in this manner. Using a particularly powerful and disturbing vignette, Van Ausdale begins her book with an example of three-year-old Carla, who uses her corporeal agency to proclaim a racial identity by relocating her nap mat.

> [Carla] picks up her cot and starts to move it to the other side of the classroom. A teacher asks what she is doing. "I need to move this," explains Carla. "Why?" asks the teacher. " 'Because I can't sleep next to a nigger," Carla says, pointing to Nicole, a four-year-old Black child on a cot nearby. "Niggers are stinky. I can't sleep next to one". (Ausdale and Feagin 2001: 1)

Evident in this example is the way in which corporeal performances can be used to confirm affiliation to an identity or group within the community, as well as to distance one from an identity or particular subgroup within the community. A similar feature is clear in the earlier example of Kyle, who asserts his "hegemonic masculinity" even when it is clearly at odds with the center's organizational and philosophical approach to interrupting traditional gender assignments.

The use of the body to try on and proclaim various identities is also evident in Kyle's appeal to his Indian ethnicity as an explanation for his commitment to only playing with boys. As Kyle informs Zac, "Well, we are Indian and we just play with boys. In my family we don't play with girls" (Skattebol 2006: 516). These sorts of assertions are commonly dismissed by educators as acts of emotional insensitivity and immaturity; they are typically not labeled as racist or sexist. Indeed, traditional developmental frameworks see children as "innocents," often as incapable of enacting consciously hurtful acts of this magnitude. While it is certainly true that children have a developing capacity to understand the ways in which their behavior reflects racist or sexist thinking prevalent in society at large, post-structuralist theorists emphasize that researchers and educators do not have to choose between seeing children as "innocent" of these sorts of harms and as racist beings. Rather, acknowledging the agency of children requires a more sophisticated analysis. The post-structuralist, co-constitutive theory asks a different question: if we assume that children use their voices and bodies in agentic ways, how might we see these incidents differently? Asking this sort of question not only repositions children's actions in school, but also many other features of the classroom and school experience. Responses to this question have implications for instruction, classroom management practices, and even the most mundane features of elementary life such as lining up, using bathroom facilities, and eating in the cafeteria.

As Holt (2004) points out, this sort of embodied identity-framing is carried out not only by children but also by adults in the classroom and contributes to the learning children experience related to stereotypes and the framing of "normal" bodies. Holt (2004) writes of a situation involving a teacher's comments to other children about Nelson, a child with learning, emotional, and communication issues. During a period of moving from one activity to lunch, Holt makes a detailed notation of the teacher's comments to other students: "I know Nelson can be a pain sometimes...you can tell the teacher. If he is being really silly, which I know he can be...you don't have to play with him if he is going to ruin things for you. I don't want him to ruin your lunchtimes" (Holt 2004: 793). While readers may be aghast at this sort of direct instruction that so consciously marginalizes another student, Holt reminds readers that adults' "stigmatising practices are most powerful when they are subtle" (Holt 2004: 793), largely because the power relations in the classroom preclude children from commenting directly on adults' practices. The teacher in this situation may claim that she was just trying to empathize with these other children about the difficulties she saw them having with Nelson. And yet, given this tacit approval to distance themselves from this child, it is easy to anticipate that these children might physically move away and adjust their proximity to Nelson, or perform other excluding gestures such as turning away when he is talking or raising their eyebrows with each other when Nelson is nearby as if to say, "oh boy...." Indeed, much of what Holt (2004) found in her observational study of two schools and the ways (dis)ability was (re)produced in these environments were the subtle and pervasive practices that reproduced notions of "normative" mind–body–socioemotional expectations. Among the most powerful Holt encountered were the rules adopted for particular games that were ubiquitous in the schools. In one school, Graham, a boy with specific learning differences, only selects Nathaniel, a boy with learning differences, for his games with the provision that Nathaniel perform only marginalized roles. Quoting Graham about Nathaniel, "whenever we say you've got to be a baddy, he says no, so we say you can't play then" (Holt 2004: 794).

Van Ausdale and Feagin (2001) further our understanding of the ways in which children enact their agency in marginalized situations. Not only does developmental theory situate children in a diminished way, but the categorical status of child works to weaken children's power, particularly with adults. Corinne, a biracial four-year-old whose mother is African and father is white and American, has such incredible difficulty explaining her racial heritage to her classmates and teachers that she eventually gives up. The following example documents both a verbal exchange between Corinne and Mike (four, white) and the gestures that correspond with their interaction. As Corinne's father arrives one day to pick her up, Mike asks,

> "Who is that?" "That's my daddy,' [Corinne] replies, beaming at her father. Mike regards the man unsmilingly, then sniffs and shakes his head vigorously. 'Uh, uh,' he declares, indicating his disbelief. Corinne stares at Mike for a moment, then says, 'Yes he is!' David [Corinne's father] looks on in amusement, a smile on his face. 'How come he ain't Black?" Mike asks Corinne. 'Because he's not,' she retorts, glaring at Mike and grabbing her father's hand. 'Uh, uh, you can't have a white dad. Black kids have Black dads,' Mike states, smiling. 'Yes I can. I do. We're from Africa.' Corinne's tone has now taken on a quieter quality, but she still frowns at Mike. 'Uh, uh,' Mike insists, 'nope'". (Ausdale and Feagin 2001: 83)

Later, a similar interaction occurred with Corinne and a staff member. Corinne and Joy were sitting together reading a book, and a picture of the pyramids was featured in the text.

> Corinne excitedly pointed to an illustration and interrupted, "Oh, those are pyramids, they're in Africa! I'm from Africa, you know,"...Corinne obviously expected agreement from the teacher, but what she got was surprising disagreement. "Oh no, honey, you're not from Africa," Joy smiled shaking her head. "You're African American." Corinne looked at her and replied, "No, I am from Africa." Corinne continues to be met with disbelief from Joy. Finally, "[f]rowning, Corinne retorts, 'No, you don't get it, I'm from Africa. My daddy is from here'". (Ausdale and Feagin 2001: 85)

In exploring the resistance Corinne found among students and staff, Van Ausdale notes that similar assertions from other students about their Asian or European ancestry were commonly believed and validated. Over time, Corinne learned a hard lesson: "Adults often do not believe what small children tell them, even if it is true" (Ausdale and Feagin 2001: 85).

Beyond the disbelief that Corinne regularly encountered, sometimes when her African origins were believed, they incurred a negative association. In another example featuring Corinne, she and another girl,

Brittany (four, white), are playing in the dress up area pretending to be mothers to some dolls in a basket. Corinne picks up the doll Brittany had been "mothering," while Brittany announces that she is getting dinner ready.

> [Brittany] immediately returns to the dress up area, snatches the doll from Corinne and says, "No, you can't take care of her. You're from Africa." Corinne frowns at her. Brittany refuses to give the doll to Corinne, who is still holding her own doll. "I don't want an African taking care of her. I want an American. You're not an American, anybody can see that," Brittany insists, frowning. Corinne frowns back, "I am too an American too. First from Africa, then America. Both." Brittany merely stalks away, leaving Corinne to stare at her. (Ausdale and Feagin 2001: 86)

Here, Brittany is using both her words and her body to affirm her status as a valid caregiver for her baby over Corinne's authority, based solely upon Brittany's (mis)perception of Corinne's racial identity. In performing such a move, Brittany indicates her higher status as an American, contrasting her whiteness against Corinne's blackness. Again, these are the kinds of incidents that teachers are likely to dismiss as hurtful but still unintentional, the result of emotional immaturity. To see children like Brittany as enacting a social message of racism and affirming her identity as an American conflicts with dominant developmental theory about children, particularly the assumed cognitive and emotional capacities of young children.

Importantly, not all examples of identity co-construction are based upon negative stereotyping and "othering." Some data suggest that leading with an (dis)abled identity can create affirming experiences with other children. If agency and the interplay between agency and identity are to be understood fully, it is critical to recognize not only incidents of negative stigmatization, but also those that construct and support a positive identity. Ali, a boy with body and learning differences, provides evidence on this point from Holt's (2004) research. In her fieldnotes, Holt records the following experience of a small group of children playing with him and his wheelchair. "Ali is wheeling around in circles with four girls holding onto the back of his wheelchair. All of the children involved are laughing and seem to be enjoying themselves" (Holt 2004: 796). Later, one of the girls involved in this excerpt, Leah, a girl with learning differences, explores her experience: " 'we play this horsy game that Ali made up—it's well, funny. You have to hold onto the back of his wheelchair and you go giddy-up [laughs]. We're pretending to be the horsies and Ali is a carriage [laughs]'" (Holt 2004: 796). As Holt (2004) notes, contrary to the "individual tragedy" paradigm of (dis)ability which would incur a negative image of the wheelchair, in this scenario Ali and the other children transform his wheelchair into an instrument for creative play. The consequences of this transformation include, at least in this setting, the notion that Ali is creative and playful, someone who makes a positive contribution to the classroom community, and thus someone who "holds a pivotal social position" (Holt 2004: 797). Employing Judith Butler's insistence on questioning categories of "natural," particularly as the term is used to partition gender into the dichotomy of "male" and "female," Holt (2004) reminds readers that bodies should not be read as "a natural given" but rather as "reproduced through identity performances which are 'tenuously constituted in time [and space]...identit[ies that are] instituted through stylised repetition of acts'" (Butler cited in Holt 2004: 787). These sorts of interactions, over time, inform the actor and others in the setting of identities—both positive and negative—that then continue to shape one's corporeal experience and agency.

From this literature, one can see that embodiment and physical gesture can be "read" in stigmatizing ways, provoking both bullying and exclusionary treatment, or in pro-social ways that frame identities as friendly and creative. While the bulk of the literature in this post-structuralist arena focuses on race, gender, and (dis)ability, partial views of social class do emerge within these stories. Holt (2004) recounts the experience of Nathaniel (the same child noted previously who was marginalized in class games by another child), who is stigmatized by other children in the class not because of his learning disabilities (as was true in the earlier example), but because he is of a different social class than some of the other children. In her conversation with Nathaniel, Holt (2004) documents the following exchange: "...children claim Nathaniel has the 'lurgies'. Nathaniel states: 'they call me names and that, and I just ignore them. They say I've got lurgies, when I ain't'" (Holt 2004: 793). Holt learns from other children that "lurgies" is an epithet of being poor. As Rosalind, a nondisabled girl in the class, reveals, "[i]t's germs, it's like, that—and if they come from—a dirty family" (Holt 2004: 793). Teachers confirm this placement of Nathaniel in a lower social class status in the classroom, which they see as a continuation of his status outside of the classroom: "those that are walking about in their Adidas trainers and all that...pick on [Nathaniel]" (Holt 2004: 793).

The picture that emerges from the insights provided by embodiment research in race and gender is very complex. Part of this complexity is driven by the different contexts in which children and adults operate and the fact that different corporeal performances have different meanings in different spaces. Added to the context issue is the notion of consciousness on the part of the corporeal actor; what she wishes to communicate with her body, messages about which she may or may not be fully aware. Then there is the issue of the actor interpreting the corporeal action: what she thinks about what she sees. Indeed, "complex" hardly seems an adjective sufficient to encapsulate all that is happening during the moment of nonverbal communication, which, readers should remember, rarely happens in the absence of other forms of communication.

And still, one of the lessons from the corporeal data on the construction of race, gender, and (dis)ability is that it is possible to, at least provisionally, apply a research lens to separate particular identity markers from one another to form more thorough understandings of how these markers are working vis-à-vis the body. So while the (re)production of embodied social class status has yet to be examined as thoroughly as some other important facets of identity, studies in race and gender suggest that such exploration is possible. Such focused attention is particularly important given the ways in which schools operate to reproduce class differences rather than ameliorate them.

Given the extensive data on how schools replicate existing social inequalities, researchers and educators interested in the workings of social class would be well advised to incorporate the co-constitutive, post-structuralist view in their work. Altering the base assumptions about children's agency and the positioning of agency in identity construction requires asking different questions about the schooling environment and embodiment, which do not emerge from traditional views of schooling. Several possible questions result from this view relative to social class. How do children of different social class status experience their schools corporeally? How do teachers "read" the bodies of children of different social class backgrounds? What are some of the instructional consequences of these (mis)interpretations by educators? Chapter 3 picks up on these questions by exploring Bourdieu's theory of social class acquisition and Lareau's theory of child-rearing practices based upon social class status.

3
Theoretical Frameworks for Understanding Social Class Corporeality

Abstract: *This chapter begins with a brief historical overview of sociology of the body as a way of framing the later treatment of Bourdieu's work on habitus, field, capital, and body hexis. Following this summary, this chapter then turns to Annette Lareau's work on child-rearing logics that correspond with social class position. After exploring Lareau's "concerted cultivation" and "accomplishment of natural growth" orientations, this chapter theorizes on how teachers might "read" the body language of children in different social class positions and the instructional consequences of such interpretations.*

Keywords: child-rearing practices; habitus; sociology of the body

Henry, Sue Ellen. *Children's Bodies in Schools: Corporeal Performances of Social Class.* New York, Palgrave Macmillan, 2014. DOI: 10.1057/9781137442635.0006.

Conceptualizing the important theoretical frameworks of Pierre Bourdieu and Annette Lareau requires some framing in the historical trajectory of sociology from which their work emerges. As such, this chapter begins with an overview of Marcel Mauss' work on techniques of the body, from which emerges Bourdieu's central focus on habitus. Following this overview of Mauss is an exploration of Bourdieu's theory of social class acquisition, which focuses on habitus and three additional central elements of Bourdieu's theory: cultural capital, field, and body hexis. Understanding these features of Bourdieu's theory sheds light on the central findings of Annette Lareau and her hallmark work on the social class influences on child-rearing practices. In this important work, she employs habitus, field, and cultural capital to reveal how social class influences language use, organization of time, interactions with institutions, and ultimately the perceptions of agency cultivated in children, via the differential "logics" of child-raising apparent in families of different social class status.

These findings highlight the ways that social class influences parental choices and behavior relative to children and the values inherent in the practices parents employ. However, one of Bourdieu's central features—body hexis—is not taken up by Lareau in any deliberate manner. Thus one aim of this chapter is to apply Bourdieu's concept of body hexis to Lareau's findings to theoretically hypothesize what sorts of embodiments one might see emerging from different social class upbringings. Using Mauss' focus on "body techniques" as a backdrop, this chapter asks what sorts of hygiene practices, uses of the body during verbal communication, and other corporeal practices are associated with the different parenting logics that align with social class status? In other words, what are the embodiments of high degrees of agency experienced by children reared in upper-class ways? What are the embodiments of the constrained agency of children reared in working-class ways? What are the implications for "self-control" that emerge from each of these pictures of embodiment?

Early sociological thinking on the body: its "absent-presence" and Marcel Mauss

The study of the body has taken different orientations in sociology throughout the evolution of the discipline. Early sociology, in its attempt to establish itself as a "legitimate" science, took a more "naturalistic" approach, conceiving of the body as a vehicle through which to observe social phenomena. The "founding fathers" of sociology—Durkheim, Weber, Simmel, and Mannheim—were largely concerned with aligning their study of the social world with the natural sciences, following the notion that humans were best understood through a nature/society dualism, with the physical body falling into the "nature" category (Shilling 2003: 22).[1] This situation led to an "absent–presence" of the body in historical sociology (Shilling 2003: 17). As Shilling (2003) maintains, early study in sociology *implicated* the body, but rarely held the body as a unit of analysis in its own right. This situation is particularly true in the sociology of education. The abstraction of the body from the mind can be observed in the sociology of education both in the liberal assimilation of "education" with intellectual development and in the social reproduction theory that characterizes schools as sites of domination without fully considering the ways in which typical school rules discipline the body of subjugated pupils. Currently, there is a surge of interest in studying the material body and the spaces bodies inhabit; these studies promise to supplant this omission with theory and empirical data.

In its earliest form, sociological theory on the body begins in the work of Emile Durkheim, Georg Simmel, and Karl Marx. Shilling (2010) maintains that among these three thinkers there exists a "centrifugal force" with regard to the body; each of these important theorists gives modern sociologists a slice of what might be important about the reciprocal relationship between the body and society. This mutual relationship between body and society rests on three principles: (1) within the body exists the source of social life; (2) the body serves as the location for social structures; and (3) the body is the means with which individuals are located within social order (Shilling 2010: 10–11).

These three ideas about the mutuality of the body and society are central to Durkheim's early work with the body in social life. Durkheim's characterization of "social facts as things" is a bit tautological but, in his editor's introduction, Lukes (1982) explains his thinking: "social facts should be regarded by the sociologist as realities, that is, as having characteristics independent of his conceptual apparatus, which can only be ascertained through empirical investigation (as opposed to *a priori* reasoning or intuition) and, in particular, through 'external' observation by means of indicators (such as legal codes, statistics, etc.), and as existing independently of individuals' wills..." (Durkheim et al. 1982: 2–3).

Durkheim began his inclusion of the body in the body–society relationship by emphasizing the power of these "social facts" on the body. He claimed that elements and patterns of society were *supra-individual* and shaped corporeal and educational consequences for people due to how they influenced individuals' thoughts, feelings, and beliefs. Durkheim stressed that because social facts were real "things" rather than mere ideas, they were "evident in the *bodily feelings, experiences, habits* and *appearances of individuals* as much as in the institutional and morphological dimensions of society" (Shilling 2010: 157, italics in original). From Durkheim's point of view then, the body is not merely a tablet upon which social norms are written; the social fact of the body also exemplifies social norms and remakes these norms via its performance of them.

According to Shilling (2010), even more critical is an underexamined premise of Durkheim's notion: social facts are generated by and emerge from the embodied foundation of society. Thus, the way in which people lead their lives is in part influenced by the ways in which they embody these "social facts." Importantly, Durkheim did not maintain that the body accepted all these facts unilaterally; he did not rule out the influence of resistance and individual will. Durkheim saw a reciprocal influence between the body and societal norms. He wanted to understand social facts as structures in society that influenced bodies, while furthering our explanation of how the uses of bodies influenced social facts that exist as localized "truths."

As the nephew of Durkheim and an important figure in sociology in his own right, Marcel Mauss was greatly influenced by this notion of social facts. Considered by Georges Condominas as "the father of French ethnography" (Fournier 2006: 1), Mauss epitomized early sociology and anthropological thinking that emphasized work with the facts over work on theories. According to biographer Marcel Fournier (2006), Mauss "shared an evolutionist conception of history and attributed a heuristic value to the study of elementary (or primative) forms of social facts" (3). First published in 1935, Mauss' "Techniques of the Body" grew out of his previous work focused on reciprocity and gift exchange in "primitive" cultures. In particular, he grew curious about the universal and particular uses of the body within and between cultures, and the rules that governed legitimate uses of the body: its moves and the influences of individual physiology on the shaping of what we would now call identity markers. Mauss suggested that this shaping, quite literally, influenced the ways in which an individual can and does move through the world and how one presents himself/herself and his/her identity.

Perhaps his most well-known example of this type of shaping is the examination of Maori women studied by ethnographer Elsdon Best in the early 1900s. Within this culture, there existed a prescribed and expected walk for girls moving into womanhood, termed *onioni*. Presence of the walk confirmed a girl's physiological and maturational anticipation of womanhood. Mauss quotes Best when he writes, "[m]others drilled their daughters in this accomplishment... and I have heard a mother say to her girl: '*Ha! Kaiore koe e onioni*' (you are not doing the *onioni)* when the young one was neglecting to practise the gait" (Best quoted in Mauss 1935/1973: 74). The implication here was that the absence of this particular gait failed to fully signify this girl as a woman in Maori culture and that the consequences of such a failure were critical with regard to the gender assignment of girls in this society. This example makes a clear case for the relationship between the movement and use of the body for social purposes. That a walk can signify one's social position as "female" in a particular culture reminds us that there is a significant interplay between the performance of certain social positions and identities (gender, sexual orientation, age) and one's membership or assignment to these social positions. The body is thus shaped by cultural significations while at the same time influencing these cultural spaces with its performances.

Mauss uses this example (and others he explores that feature bodily actions such as running, digging, and the position of the hands during walking) to suggest that these uses of the body are indeed best understood as "techniques of the body." Working from Durkheim's reciprocal position between the body and culture, Mauss offers an extended tripartite understanding of the body in culture. He maintains that one cannot fully understand the use of the body in a particular way in a particular culture unless one sees that the body simultaneously signifies mechanical, psychological, and sociological properties. The body represents a physiological set of conditions, at the same time that it represents a set of psychological conditions to its user, while simultaneously representing some sociological facets to the social world in which it acts and performs.

Based on these principles, Mauss attempted to construct a taxonomy of some of the features one would study (an ethnology) to understand these overlapping physiological–psychological–sociological conditions of and in the body. Focusing on those bodily techniques that indicated membership in the adult ranks, Mauss began to sketch his taxonomy focusing on sleep, waking and notions of rest, and repetitive movements such as climbing, trampling, walking, jumping, running, dancing, and swimming for details about the physiological elements that could be understood in light of their psychological and sociological components. Mauss also focused on "forceful" movements, such as pushing, pulling, lifting, throwing, holding, and the way of holding an object being thrown, as well as hygiene practices, practices in eating, consumption, and drinking patterns. By directing researchers' attention to these physical performances, Mauss hoped to elucidate the relationship between how people used their bodies and the reciprocal, psychological and sociological consequences of these uses. Linking the physiological performance of the body with its psychological and sociological effects was at the heart of Mauss' notion of "techniques of the body." Techniques of the body, "the ways in which from society to society, men [sic] know how to use their bodies" could shed light on the social station one lived in, one's perception of this condition, and elucidate how the body was implicated in the construction and reproduction of this social situation (Farnell 2000: 401).

Mauss suggested that, collectively, these actions underscored the bodily demonstration of one's *habitus*, by which he emphasized the social nature of embodied action. When discussing *habitus*, Mauss acknowledges that while there may be a slight variation between individuals, the more critical variations—those that sociologists should be interested in pursuing—were those across cultures. Important for a contemporary application to social class, Mauss suggested that "[t]hese 'habits' do not just vary within individual...they vary especially between societies, education, properties and fashions, prestiges. In them we should see the techniques and work of collective and individual practical reason..." (Mauss 1973: 73). Thus, Mauss meant to distinguish between habit, which he saw as an individual-level phenomenon, and habitus, which suggested variation between groups. As Crossley notes when exploring Mauss' understanding, "we all have individual habits but habitus are social facts, in Durkheim's (1982) sense" (Crossley 2013: 40).

Habitus, a term now utilized throughout sociological literature, has a variety of meanings. For Mauss, the key understanding about habitus is summarized by Crossley (2013): "the image [of habitus] Mauss conjures, [is] of actors in different social communities acquiring from those communities the dispositions and skills constitutive of practical reason"

(Crossley 2013: 4). This social facticity permeates Bourdieu's use of the term as well, and underscores the central positioning of this crucial concept. According to Farnell (2000), Bourdieu capitalized on Mauss' early observation of the reciprocal nature of body and society vis-à-vis habitus, what Farnell calls Mauss' "programmatic suggestions about the constitutive role of embodied action in the construction of class and status" (401), by conceiving of a fortified notion of habitus that did more theoretical heavy lifting than Mauss' early use of the term.

While not without his critics, Bourdieu remains a central figure in the ways in which sociologists attempt to understand and use the concept of habitus. As Farnell (2000) observes, Bourdieu's conception is at times problematic. Sociologist Nick Crossley acknowledges that Bourdieu's work on habitus is consistently evolving over time, such that there is no one definitive definition of this essential concept that emerges (Crossley 2013). And yet, Bourdieu remains at the core of studies focusing on social class and the embodiment of social class structures. As Crossley observes, "habitus is an everyday term in much contemporary sociology largely because of its use in the work of Bourdieu" (Crossley 2013: 36).

Bourdieu: habitus, field, capital, and body hexis

Similar to Mauss, Pierre Bourdieu (1 August 1930–23 January 2002) is hard to pin down to a singular disciplinary home. His writing and theorizing offer significant contributions to sociology and social theory writ large. He is most often categorized as a French sociologist, whose career spans some 30 years of copious academic work in sociology, anthropology, and philosophy. His influence is seen throughout these disciplines, as well as in subfields within these academic areas. Four main concepts are essential to the understanding of the ways in which embodiment works: habitus, social field, cultural capital, and body hexis.

Habitus

Habitus is a common, often imprecisely used, term. According to sociologist Richard Jenkins, the Latin word *habitus* refers "to a habitual or typical condition, state or appearance, particularly of the body" (Jenkins quoted in Farnell 2000: 399). Early uses of the word related to medical conditions associating certain bodily conditions with particular disease states ("Habitus, N." 2013).

Starting from Mauss' idea of habitus as a set of "acquired abilities," Bourdieu articulates habitus as a set of "dispositions which incline agents to act and react in certain ways" (Bourdieu 1991: 12). Bourdieu maintains that habitus offers individuals an insight into how to act and respond throughout situations they encounter in their lives; it gives individuals a "feel for the game." Such "conditionings" are associated with particular classes, as his work in *Distinction* (1984) so aptly supports, by gathering copious data on a variety of matters of taste and preference varying by social class strata (among them, preferences for singers, furniture choices, newspaper reading rates, etc.).

One comes by the habitus through experience with the structures of social life and through direct inculcation and teaching, which characterizes habitus as "inculcated, structured, durable, generative and transposable" (Bourdieu 1991: 12). In essence, habitus is what we think is "normal" and expected behavior for people "like us," however we define our group affinity. Calling upon the foundation of Mauss, Bourdieu distinguishes between habit and habitus, suggesting that while habit embeds behavior in the body and conceals the reason we respond in certain ways, habitus does not "[rule] out that the responses of the habitus may be accompanied by a strategic calculation tending to perform in a conscious mode the operation that the habitus performs quite differently, namely an estimation of chances presupposing transformation of the past effect into an expected objective" (Bourdieu 1990: 53). As such, Bourdieu acknowledges that one of the ways habitus is reformed is through calculated, novel responses to new situations and issues. This notion of habitus as both an enduring structure and a flexible one is controversial; critics of Bourdieu suggest that, at times, his description of habitus is too structuring to account for human agency (Farnell 2000). Indeed, in many ways, there are multiple conceptions of habitus offered by Bourdieu over the course of his writings, and one consequence is that interpretations are likely to conflict with one another. It is certainly true that, in some statements about habitus, Bourdieu seems to emphasize the structuring structures that account for the firm (though not solidified) nature of habitus. In *The Logic of Practice* (1990), an important text for theoretically grounding his central concepts, Bourdieu writes,

> the conditionings associated with a particular class of conditions of existence produce habitus, systems of durable, transposable dispositions, structured structures predisposed to function as structuring structures, that is, as principles which generate and organize practices and representations that can

be objectively adapted to their outcomes without presupposing a conscious aiming at ends or an express mastery of the operations necessary in order to attain them. (Bourdieu 1990: 53)

And yet, Bourdieu also emphasizes throughout his work with relative consistency that habitus is not a sheer mechanistic response—it is not habit in its more narrow form—but actions that acknowledge the idea that freedom is shaped and influenced by conditions that reflect reasonable limits and constraints on our behavior, much of which are influenced by social class. "Through the habitus, the structure of which it is the product governs practice, not along the paths of mechanical determinism, but within the constraints and limits initially set on its inventions" (Bourdieu 1990: 55). Such critiques account for Bourdieu's continual revision of the term throughout his vast career (Crossley 2013).

Field

Bourdieu describes field as the social milieu in which an actor is situated. Fields suggest social institutions (home, school, public locations, disciplines of study) where there are norms for behavior implied, often without the benefit of overt teaching about these norms. Instead, signals for the expectations for behavior are embedded in these fields. Indeed, Bourdieu wrote extensively about a variety of "fields" including material spaces such as economics, politics, and other social realms, as well as institutional situations. The embedded norms in each of these spaces constitute a habitus of the field and, because individuals operate in these fields, there is by definition a relational orientation between an individual's perception or understanding of a field influenced by habitus and the habitus of the field in which the individual is operating. As Thompson suggests in his editor's introduction to Bourdieu's *Language and Symbolic Power* (1991), "...when individuals act, they always do so in specific social contexts or settings. Hence particular practices or perceptions should be seen, not as the product of the habitus as such, but as the product of the *relation between* the habitus, on the one hand, and the specific social contexts or 'fields' within which individuals act on the other" (14). Consistent with a post-structuralist, co-constitutive orientation, Bourdieu emphasizes the idea that individuals and spaces they inhabit are in constant negotiation.

In several of his most well-known works, Bourdieu outlines this important relationship between habitus and field. The field is where the "feel for the game" takes place; and it is clear that one needs a field, a social location in which to have this "feel for the game" either come alive or fall flat. Being able to anticipate the norms of behavior and the hidden expectations of a field is what Bourdieu means by having a "feel for the game." In discussing the power of this phrase, Bourdieu observes, "this phrase... gives a fairly accurate idea of the almost miraculous encounter between the *habitus* and a field, between incorporated history and objectified history, which makes possible the near-perfect anticipation of the future inscribed in all the concrete configurations on the pitch or board" (Bourdieu 1990: 66, italics in original). When this "near-perfect" alignment occurs, it sustains for the actor and others in the field that what is taking place makes sense and is the "right" thing to happen. As Bourdieu writes, "...native membership in a field implies a feel for the game...[and] the capacity for practice anticipation...[makes] everything that takes place in it [seem] *sensible*: full of sense and objectively directed in a judicious direction" (Bourdieu 1990: 66, italics in original). It is in fact the "naturalness" of such attributions that conceals the habitus in a field as a set of shared expectations and agreements between people, obscured coordinations that have evolved over time, often without overt conscious attention. Thus part of the power in the "near-perfect" overlap between habitus that middle-class children bring with them to school emerges from the fact that such situations of overlap make it increasingly difficult to (1) see other sensible options and (2) act in other sensible ways. Bourdieu (1990) observes that it is only in the most conscious of moments, asking considered questions about why we do the things we do in the way we do them, that habitus and field can become transparent. Otherwise, he maintains, the force and power of habitus remain unconscious and largely unquestioned.

In such cases, the relationship between habitus and field becomes automatic, becoming games in themselves. Importantly, learning the rules of the game is not an act on which one consciously boards, but rather "one is born into the game, with the game; and the relation of investment, *illusio*, investment is made more total and unconditional by the fact that it is unaware of what it is" (Bourdieu 1990: 67, italics in original). It is at this point that beliefs become the mainstay of habitus developed in a field, internalized within person and field, and come to be extraordinarily difficult to dislodge. Some beliefs that accrue in the field are more solidified than others; Bourdieu (1990) claims that beliefs learned early on are particularly resistant to questioning, thereby ensuring the reproduction of habitus.

> The earlier a player enters the game and the less he is aware of the associated learning (the limiting case being, of course, that of someone born into, born with the game), the greater is his ignorance of all that is tacitly granted through his investment in the field and his interest in its very existence and perpetuation and in everything that is played for in it, and his unawareness of the unthought presuppositions that the game produces and endlessly reproduces, thereby reproducing the conditions of its own perpetuation. (67)

This "anticipation"—being able to properly predict the future and its obligations for one's voice, body, and actions in the field—is essential to the notion of self-control. Failure to anticipate the future accurately, however, is often conscious to actors as well as powerful observers, such as teachers. When powerful actors in a field see that others have failed to know what is to happen, they are likely to attribute to the actor this amorphous condition called lack of "self-control." What happens to individuals when failure occurs has been the subject of many interesting qualitative research projects (Horvat and Antonio 1999; MacLeod 2008). Necessary for understanding these successes and failures is not only the habitus of individual actors, but also the habitus of the field in which they are residing.

While the notion of "field" is relatively straightforward, it is a critical feature of Bourdieu's theory of social class. One of the important components of field is that it foregrounds the idea that not all resources individuals bring with them to various social fields will be acknowledged as assets. That is, various dispositions that individuals bring as a result of habitus will not be equally recognized or valued in various fields, due to the fact that fields also have habitus associated with them. This concept brings us to Bourdieu's notion of capital—the resources individuals use to play the game of the field in which they are in.

Capital

According to Bourdieu, there are several forms of capital: resources that actors draw upon in interaction in a variety of fields. These resources are framed by habitus; different types and expressions of capital are acquired in different circumstances, largely influenced by the social class of the individual. Among these forms of capital are economic capital (financial assets such as material wealth, stocks, property, inheritance and the like), as well as cultural capital, which Bourdieu defines as "knowledge, skills and other cultural acquisitions, as exemplified by educational or technical qualifications" (Bourdieu 1991: 14). There is also symbolic capital, for example, "accumulated prestige or honour" (Bourdieu 1990: 14) that often comes as a result of experiences in various fields (such as prestigious schooling or being a child in a wealthy family). A related form of cultural and symbolic capital is linguistic capital, "the capacity to produce expressions *a propos*, for a particular market" (Bourdieu 1991: 18). These resources assist individuals in "playing the game" in various fields, and help actors do the important work of anticipating what behaviors, verbal, and nonverbal communications will be expected in the face of novel situations. These forms of capital shape the degree to which individuals feel a sense of "fit" in a particular field—they inform the extent to which the ways of being in the world that an actor "naturally" brings with him or her adhere with the expectations of a particular field or social location. As such, access to a variety of forms of capital within each of these varieties can offer individuals greater opportunities in various fields.

In exploring the centrality of linguistic capital, Bourdieu suggests that there are two critical elements at work. One feature is the particular linguistic expectations and conventions that cohere with habitus, which result in an actor's proclivity to produce speech in such a way that conforms to the expectations of the field. The other critical feature of linguistic capital focuses on the "structures of the linguistic market" which shape the ways in which actors conform to behavioral and comportment expectations that exist in particular fields (Bourdieu 1991: 37). So powerful is this pull to conform that individuals self-censor in order to try to meet the expectations of the field (Bourdieu 1991: 19).

There are three important caveats about capital. The first is that while Bourdieu uses economic terms throughout his writings to refer to capital associated with various fields, such as "market, capital, profit" (Bourdieu 1990: 14), he does not mean to be economically deterministic with their interpretation. Second, one must remember that all habitus conditions have some particular forms of economic, symbolic, and cultural capital. Families living in poverty have economic, cultural, and symbolic capital, albeit different kinds than families living in wealth. Thus, it is important to understand that capital is best understood as differences in *kind* between different fields (such as different social class positions), which then is accumulated, learned and internalized vis à vis habitus.

Third, different fields value different forms of cultural, economic, and symbolic capital differently. For example, early learners come to school having sat on multiple surfaces (chairs, cushions, couches, floor) for all sorts of activities such as using handheld computer devices, reading books, watching television, and playing with games and toys. But when these same children begin to attend school, learning to sit in a chair with proper posture becomes a primary aim, as proper posture is assumed to be associated with clear handwriting (Feder and Majnemer 2007; Ishihara, Dake, Kashihara, and Ishihara 2010) and other ideas about attentiveness that are reinforced through a particular sitting position.[2]

Body hexis

Body hexis refers to the way in which language (broadly conceived), shaped by the habitus, is inscribed in and on the body. Body hexis is the corporeal performance of one's habitus, which is influenced by social class conditions growing up, and the fields in which one finds himself. As Bourdieu observes, body hexis is both conscious and unconscious to the actor, a form of performance that incorporates "[t]he close correspondence between the uses of the body, of language and no doubt also of time"...the mechanism through which "groups inculcate the virtues which are the transfigured form of their necessity, and...the 'choices' constitutive of a relationship with the economic and social world are incorporated in the form of durable frames that are partly beyond the grasp of consciousness and will" (Bourdieu 1991: 89).[3] Body hexis describes the way in which beliefs developed in one's habitus come to be corporeally performed and lived out.

As such, this concept suggests that the body serves as another form of communication about the habitus and social status one inhabits. Bourdieu claims that the anticipation of the various expectations of habitus and field implicates the body in a "practical quasi-corporeal sense of reality" (Bourdieu 1991: 81), and maintains that both self-assurance (when the habitus of individual overlaps with the habitus of field) and self-censorship and silence (when the habitus of the individual diverges from the habitus of field) are experienced corporeally. Indeed, Bourdieu describes habitus as "embodied history" (Bourdieu 1990: 56). Elaborating, Bourdieu writes that habitus is ingrained in the body "in such a way that [the structured dispositions of habitus] endure through the life history of the individual, operating in a way that is pre-conscious and hence not readily amenable to conscious reflection and modification" (Bourdieu 1991: 13). Bourdieu goes so far as to suggest that an institution (such as school or the family) is only possible to the extent that it can impart a corporeal logic for how to be in it, or as Bourdieu writes, "only if it is durably objectified not only in this, that is, in the logic, transcending individual agents, or a particular field, but also in bodies..." (Bourdieu 1990: 58). In other words, an institution's legitimacy is based in part in its capacity to make its principles so natural as to be above critique and inquiry. One of the ways in which fields accomplish this task is by making claims upon not only the minds of individuals but also their bodies. Hence, from Bourdieu's point of view, it is not only *what* we say that marks our habitus and class circumstances, but also *how* we say it. As Bourdieu observes when discussing the importance of inculcation in institutions,

> [naturalization in inculcation] can also tend to inculcate durable dispositions like class tastes, which, being the principle behind the "choice" of outward signs expressing social position, like clothes, but also bodily hexis or language, make all social agents the carriers of distinctive signs...More convinc[ing are] the incorporated signs (such as manners, ways of speaking—accents—, ways of walking or standing—gait, posture, bearing—, table manners, etc. and taste) which underlie the production of all practices aimed, intentionally or not, both signifying...social position. (Bourdieu 1991: 123)

Additionally, one of the ways that an individual demonstrates being part of social institutions (such as schools) is by complying with the corporeal performance expectations that govern such spaces. For outsiders, this is particularly difficult because these "rules" are often covertly maintained and implicit rather than explicitly anchored.

The search for corporeal features that signify one's social position harkens back to Mauss and his work to categorize the variances between different populations. Interestingly, current research supports the idea that these sorts of nonverbal gestures are how adults communicate their social class status. For example, Kraus and Keltner's (2009) work verifies that adults communicate their social class status nonverbally. Upper-socioeconomic status adults do so through "disengagement" behaviors such as doodling during conversations. Lower-socioeconomic status adults offer more "engagement" behaviors such as eye contact and nodding at a speaker. By viewing these differences, observers accurately predicted family income, maternal education, and subjective socioeconomic status (Kraus and Keltner 2009). This research suggests that the cumulative influence of embodied social class status on childhood and early adulthood results in a repertoire of adult, embodied, social class gestures that observers can (and do) use to accurately predict social class status. It is important to remember, however, that corporeal behavior is not "caused" purely by one's habitus and body hexis—rather, these dispositions are brought to a social field, which also exerts its own pressures with regard to the norms and expectations associated with it, that then influences the behavior of the individual. As Bourdieu (1991) observes "...particular practices or perceptions should be seen, not as the product of the habitus as such, but as the product of the *relation between* the habitus, on the one hand, and the specific social contexts or 'fields' within which individuals act, on the other" (Bourdieu 1991: 14, italics in original). As such, we are reminded of the power and influence of fields to sway behavior through imposition of norms and expectations. Such influence is likely to be particularly powerful in the case of young learners.

Body hexis is also supported in the findings from recent literature on the importance of subjective social class rank. Subjective social class rank refers to one's subjective assessment of his/her social class rank within a particular location or social situation. Contrasted with subjective social class rank is the notion of objective social class rank, most often measured by income, education, and occupational prestige. Social science in this area often asks participants to rank their social class standing on a ten-rung ladder representing society (Adler, Epel, Castellazzo, & Ickovics 2000). Research reveals that subjective social class rank has a powerful predictive value relative to evidence of ill-health (Singh-Manoux, Adler, & Marmot 2003), not explained by objective measures of wealth, education, and occupation alone. For instance, Goodman et al. (2001) found that after altering the ten-rung ladder for an adolescent audience and asking young people to offer their subjective social class rank relative to their school community, subjective social class rank was predictive of depressive symptoms (with higher self-ranked individuals experiencing fewer depressive symptoms), as well as obesity rates (with lower self-ranked individuals experiencing greater obesity than their higher self-ranked counterparts). This research suggests that while the frequent social science measure of socioeconomic status vis-à-vis education level, occupational prestige, and wealth is important, measuring subjective social class rank can also shed significant light on the influence of social class on a variety of corporeal factors.

One critique of Bourdieu's notion theory of habitus, capital, field, and body hexis is that it does not go far enough to explain its acquisition (Noble and Watkins 2003). As we will see in the next section, Annette Lareau offers some important insights into this question, exploring the ways in which child-rearing practices are framed by the social class positioning of parents and the consequences that child-rearing practices have on children's sense of themselves as either objects or subjects in their world. In other words, Lareau offers readers a window into the inculcative practices that motivate the acquisition of habitus in young children.

Lareau and the influence of social class on child-rearing practices

Described as an "instant classic," Annette Lareau's (2003/2011) book, *Unequal Childhoods: Class, Race, and Family Life*, explores the ways in which social class influences child-rearing practices utilized by parents. Employing Bourdieu's theoretical framework of habitus, cultural capital, and the field of the home, her naturalistic research methodology is based on work with 12 families, whom themselves were part of a larger study of 88 children from middle-class, working-class, and poor backgrounds. Lareau's ethnographic research with these 12 families included over 20 visits with each family in the space of about one month. Lareau and her research assistants spent one overnight with each family, and recorded the rhythms of family life as their visits unfolded.

Lareau utilized Bourdieu's theory of how social class shapes life experience, starting from the assumption that individuals "of different social locations are socialized differently" (Lareau 2003: 275). As such, Lareau uses the terms that Bourdieu developed to explore how middle-class children learn the "rules of the game" (Lareau 2003: 6) and how children of working-class and poor status learn to feel ineffectual in shaping social structures in dominant fields (such as school). Significantly, Lareau uses terminology of cultural capital, habitus, and field in her thorough explanation and analysis of these children's lives, but admits to having administered a "partial" employment of Bourdieu's work (Lareau 2003: 276). One primary omission in Lareau's analysis is an exploration of the ways in which children *embody* their social class status vis-à-vis the child-rearing "logic" they experience. In other words, what might the corporeal performances of children raised in these "logics" look like? This important question is still open for empirical study and exploration; however, weaving together Mauss' influence on Bourdieu, Bourdieu's consideration of the body hexis and social class, and Lareau's detailed understanding of the phenomenological experience of children in their social class homes offers some hypotheses.

What result from this vast amount of data are two "logics" of child-rearing. Middle-class parents exhibit the logic of "concerted cultivation," while the child-rearing practices of working-class and poor parents cohere around the logic of "accomplishment of natural growth." These logics are most evident in the family's orientation to time, language use, and interventions with institutions. Collectively, these class-based differences in child-rearing patterns result in differential understandings of the self, either as "entitled" (in middle-class homes) or "constrained" (in working-class and poor homes) (Lareau 2003: 6–7).

Concerted cultivation: a story of empowerment

The logic of concerted cultivation centers on the premise that the role of the parent is to create an adult through their parenting practices. As such, choices about rearing practices with regard to the organization of time, language use, and interactions with institutions follow the core principle that children should practice skills that they will use and need as resources when they become adults. Middle-class parents in Lareau's study frequently cited the importance of being involved in activities and learning to manage time and multiple responsibilities through participation in multiple curricular and cocurricular experiences. Concerted cultivation parents advanced the notion that organized sports teaches children the benefits of competition and to become a "team player," which prepares children for the performance-based assessments present in school. One middle-class parent observed the importance of sports in teaching perseverance,

> Last week or the week before [my son] came down with semi-weepy eyes [saying] that homework was too difficult. So we said, "You know, it's like a soccer game. What do you do if you're playing in a soccer game? Do you start crying and say you can't do it? No, you know this is going to be a hard one, so you just try harder." So he went back upstairs and did his homework. (Lareau 2003: 62)

Indeed, adult-organized, supervised activities were an essential component of the middle-class time structure. Of the 12 families included in Lareau's study, organized activities among the middle-class children outpaced those of working-class children nearly 2:1; the ratio was more than 3:1 when compared to poor children (Lareau 2003: 283). Overall, family life in these homes appeared crowded and rushed. Parents spent considerable time and money shuttling children to multiple activities outside of school, all in the name of constructing a young adult who was learning important lessons of dedication and commitment and time management skills.

The concerted cultivation orientation to language extends this thematic emphasis on preparing for adulthood. In middle-class homes, language exchanges between parents and children centered on the logical use of language, extended rationale for various positions, and linguistic "sparring." Words were often enjoyed for their own sake, emphasizing the "intrinsic pleasure" in words and "alternate meanings" afforded to various words. Consistent with Bernstein's (1973) work, language was the medium middle-class children and parents used for declaring positions and negotiating for particular interests. This negotiation for interests featured prominently, in exchanges with parents and other adult authority figures. Lareau uses Alexander Williams, one of the middle-class children in her study, as an example of this linguistic orientation:

> ...rather than order or direct children, middle-class parents would offer children 'choices' for decisions. But then, these parents would unobtrusively guide their children toward the choice that they thought was preferable. In choosing fast food or in choosing a book for a summer reading list,...Ms. Williams would ask Alexander what he wanted, but then would suggest one or two options as the most appropriate. Often, when Alexander felt he was making his own decisions, he was in fact following his mother's suggestions. (Lareau 2003: 120)

These self-advocacy language skills were also practiced with other adults in children's lives. Drawing on another example from Alexander Williams, Lareau describes an interaction with him and his mother in preparation for an upcoming doctor's appointment. Exemplifying the relaxed and comfortable interaction with authority figures that underscored the position of concerted cultivation, Ms. Williams says to Alexander, "Alexander, you should be thinking of questions you might want to ask the doctor. You can ask him anything you want. Don't be shy. You can ask anything" (Lareau 2003: 124).

Lareau maintains that the organization of a child's time largely at the direction of adults, coupled with the linguistic capital afforded children in their interactions with these adults, leads children of concerted cultivation to see themselves as equal actors in the company of adult authority figures. Lareau references the previous interaction between Alexander Williams and his doctor noting how his mother has set up the interaction as a communication between equals ("you can ask anything"), and tacitly suggests to Alexander that his own questions are of at least equal value to the doctor's questions for him about his health. In other words, Alexander and middle-class children like him have learned (1) that their opinions matter, (2) to use "proper" grammar and language when addressing adults, and (3) to pull evidence together to support their claims (Lareau 2003: 129). Such skills represent dominant linguistic capital of the upper class and mark Alexander as a member of this field. Bourdieu affirms that these are the kinds of skills that the upper class are likely to marshal for their own interests. According to Bourdieu, "... difference in terms of accent, grammar and vocabulary... are indices of the social positions of speakers and reflections of the quantities of linguistic capital (and other capital) which they possess" (1991: 18).

Concerted cultivation also emerged in the ways in which middle-class parents interacted with social institutions such as school. Lareau's research suggests that middle class parents (largely mothers) were "often very interventionist" with their children's complaints (with varying levels of success), and sent the message to their children that they should self-advocate and "not take no for an answer" (Lareau 2003: 163). From the logic of concerted cultivation, a child's problem is a parent's problem, and Lareau maintains that there are two advantages for children that result from this approach to problem solving. One is that children have a more individualized experience of school, health care, and other significant institutions; second and most important, children learn to *expect* such individualized treatment. Lareau cites the intervention of Ms. Marshall, mother of Stacey, as a classic example of this approach. Having changed gymnastics classes, Stacy finished a lesson one day visibly upset by having been corrected by the instructor. After speaking unsuccessfully with the instructor, Ms. Marshall called the owner of the gymnastics school the following day and arranged for Stacey to switch into an advanced class that was, technically, already full. Lareau maintains that Stacey sees and experiences the advantages of pursuing one's concerns to their full degree and concludes that "such learning as a child has the potential to be a tremendous lifelong asset" (Lareau 2003: 173). Lareau posits that such exchanges lead children of concerted cultivation to perceive themselves as entitled to independent rights and to have their own expectations of exchanges with adult authority figures. This position extends to the institutions these adults represent, namely school authorities.

This sense of children's rights, coupled with middle-class parents' practice of intervening on behalf of their children, results in a sense of entitlement among children that carries with it a set of behaviors that secures their position of unequal advantage in institutional settings. As Lareau (2003) observes, "there are signs that middle-class children benefit, in ways that are invisible to them and to their parents, from the degree of similarity between the cultural repertoires in the home and those standards adopted by institutions" (237). From this position, not only does the logic of school feel familiar to middle-class children—they bring with them a "feel for the game" as Bourdieu would suggest—but these children have internalized a sense of themselves that establishes that their needs, desires, and experiences are important indicators of how the school is performing.

Lareau, however, remains cautious about concluding that such advantages mean that concerted cultivation is a superior parenting logic. Indeed, she makes clear that other factors evident in concerted cultivation, such as whining among children, lack of time spent with extended family, and lack of opportunity for children to have unstructured play periods, leave unexamined some of the negative side effects their child-rearing experiences may incur. Concerted cultivation is a powerful parenting logic largely because it conforms to the dominant habitus and use of various forms of capital typical of institutions, particularly school, but not because it is "better" in any sort of objective sense.

This overlap between habitus of school and home has some important consequences for the central feature of self-control. To use Bourdieu's words, concerted cultivation creates a sense of "native membership" in the field of schooling which "implie[s] a feel for the game in the sense of a capacity for practical anticipation of the 'upcoming' future contained in the present, eveything that takes place in it seems *sensible*: full of sense and objectively directed in a judicious direction" (Bourdieu 1990: 66). Embodied knowledge and body knowledge, such as how to shake hands, how to look adults in the eye when communicating, how to listen for directions, how to gesture to another to indicate understanding, are comprised in the corporeal rituals of early schooling. These rituals normalize being "kept apart" and "keeping hands to the self" (Leafgren 2009/2011) and the teacher-led rite-of-passage rituals signaling who has mastered the moves of "hegemony of technical rationality" implicit in elementary classrooms across the nation (McCadden 1997: 240). In other words, "self control" results when children raised in concerted cultivation find the habitus of school familiar, amplifying their power of anticipation in the schooling context.

Accomplishment of natural growth: a story of constraint

Lareau's research also details the parenting practices of those from working-class and poor backgrounds, which Lareau characterizes as the logic of "accomplishment of natural growth." From this point of view, parents understand children as different sorts of persons than adults, who consequently have different sorts of activities, ways of using their time, responsibilities, and expectations. Different from their upper-middle-class counterparts, working-class and poor parents do not profess that children are "adults in the making," but rather persons who are living a particular moment in their lives that at some point will indeed end, but whose character is different from adults. As such, parents using this logic believe that children should organize their own games, spend considerable time in play, and generally "hang out" with siblings and extended family. The parent's role is to offer love and meet children's needs for shelter, food, clothing, and supporting them getting to school.

In describing the differences between parents using these two logic bases, Lareau is careful to remind readers that both sets of parents are making numerous choices day in and day out that provide care to children: selecting their food, making sure they are properly clothed, supervising hygiene, asking about homework, and offering affection (albeit often in different forms). What distinguishes accomplishment of natural growth parents from those using concerted cultivation is the organization of home time, language use in the home, and relational interactions with institutions, all of which are deeply influenced by the core difference between these two logic positions in how parents view childhood.

Children raised in accomplishment of natural growth homes participated in organized activities outside of school, but did so at much lower rates than concerted cultivation children, and often arranged these opportunities on their own. Parents endorsed these activities for their children, but did not see their parenting role as including the direct encouragement and supervising of these opportunities. Katie Brindle is such an example. A white, 4th grade girl, Katie operates as many of the working-class and poor children in Lareau's study. She is a responsible, "bouncy" (86) girl whose family spends time watching television together, talking about hair, manicures, hair color, and styles. Katie commonly fixes herself a snack when she returns home from school at the end of the day, and has organized two after-school activities for herself: she sings in a choir for one hour once a week and, on some Friday evenings, she participates in a Christian youth program (Lareau 2003: 87). Compared to Alexander Williams and the other concerted cultivation children in the study, Katie's schedule has far more discretionary time, which she commonly fills with playing with Barbies, watching television, playing Nintendo, and some "long periods of practicing the development of herself as a beauty object" (Lareau 2003: 87).

Katie's mother sees her responsibility to support Katie's activities, mostly by offering verbal endorsement, but not for the purpose of cultivating an innate sense of Katie's internal talents or desires for occupations or hobbies in the future. Ms. Brindle's extended family, all of whom live nearby, are well integrated into their home life; Katie takes a ten-minute bus ride to her grandmother's house on her own on a weekly basis. As Lareau (2003) maintains, "it is her extended family that provides the structure around which she and her children organize their lives" (87) a distinct difference from concerted cultivation that prioritizes children's activities in the family schedule. While Ms. Brindle supports Katie's participation in these activities, demonstrated by spending money on the required outfit for a performance and inquiring about how they are going, she does not discuss Katie's singing in these activities as a lead-up to some further talent that Katie will likely use as an adult. She does not speak to Katie in a way that encourages Katie to develop her singing as a "formal talent" (Lareau 2003: 100). Ms. Brindle suggests several benefits of Katie's participation when she comments,

> It's just that it gives her something to do and to be with other kids and that makes her feel better, to do that, instead of being home and being bored...It makes her happy, you know. It gives her something to do. I have no complaints. (Lareau 2003: 100)

Consistent with the logic of accomplishment of natural growth, Ms. Brindle sees her primary responsibilities as making sure that Katie is prepared for and attending school, is well fed and loved. Lareau notes that while all families practicing accomplishment of natural growth seemed willing to observe children's activities occasionally or to join them in a game, "adults in working-class and poor families make relatively few interventions in children's leisure activities, especially compared to the level of involvement we observed in middle-class homes" (Lareau 2003: 98). Lareau observes that special after-school activities and children's play did not seem extraordinary to working-class and poor parents. "Most working-class and poor parents did not consider children's activities as consequential, or more specifically, as something that *ought* to involve adult time or energy. In their view, children's activities are something they do with one another, not with adults" (Lareau 2003: 98). Such a position meant that adult activities were different from children's activities, resulting in two different but often compatible worlds within one household.

Coupled with the lack of access to discretionary resources (such as markers, paper, scissors, rulers, costumes, and other craft supplies), Lareau observes that Ms. Brindle likely feels the burden of her poverty in ways that seriously curtail her ability to spend money in ways consistent with those of concerted cultivation parents. Importantly, however, Lareau notes that it is not simply the differences in access to financial resources that distinguish these parenting logics from one another. She maintains,

> the economic burdens are formidable and are compounded by her daughter's health problems. But, large as those problems are, they probably account only in part for the approach Ms. Brindle takes. Even if she had less on her mind, Katie's mother probably would not substantially change how she views her daughter's talents or alter her response to Katie's bids for adult attention. She tried hard to meet her children's basic needs. ... But nurturing her children's creative development is not something she sees as her responsibility. In general, she believes that children's play is for children. (Lareau 2003: 101)

Economic deprivation was a considerable influence on the ways in which language was used among accomplishment of natural growth parents and children, and offered a striking distinction from families of concerted cultivation. Using Harold McAllister as her example, Lareau describes the many relatives who both live with and frequent the McAllister home. Beyond Harold's immediate family of five, there are six other family members who live with the McAllister's. The numerous people, coupled with the McAllister's enrollment in AFDC (Aid to Families with Dependent Children), means that food is consistently in short supply. Lareau maintains that because living conditions are precarious, language plays a very practical role in assuring physical care, satisfactory shelter, and clothing, and teaching right from wrong. Rather than using language to assert Harold's personal power, such as Ms. Williams's support of her son Alex's discussion with his doctor, Ms. McAllister does not encourage Harold to elaborate verbally, nor does she use language to "enrich his vocabulary, cultivate his verbal (or physical) talents, cajole him, or attempt to persuade him to act in particular ways" (Lareau 2003: 139). Indeed, for accomplishment of natural growth parents, language is instrumental and they "[expect] prompt, respectful compliance" (Lareau 2003: 139).

Beyond the difference in the purpose of language, actual differences in sentence structure and vocabulary were also found in Lareau's study. Because language did not involve extended discussions, sentences were shorter, simpler words were more frequently used, negotiations were infrequent, and "word play" characteristic in concerted cultivation homes was not present in accomplishment of natural growth homes. Lareau observes that the freedom children experienced in their daily schedules extended to their communication, but they were not specifically encouraged to speak or to use words to express themselves. "The overall effect is that language serves as a practical conduit of daily life, not as a tool for cultivating reasoning skills or a resource to plumb for ways to express feelings or ideas" (146). An exemplar of this sort of verbal focus is Ms. McAllister's single-word exhortations to her children to organize the use of one bathroom in her apartment among the 11 individuals who live there. "Ms. McAllister sends the children to wash up by pointing to a child, saying, 'Bathroom,' and handing him or her a washcloth. Wordlessly, the designated child gets up and goes to the bathroom to take a shower" (Lareau 2003: 147).

Children from these homes were obedient overall; there were far fewer protests and less whining among the working-class and poor children when compared to their middle-class counterparts. Lareau observes that it is perhaps because of the expectation of children's obedience that parents did not routinely offer explanation for their directives, as was common in the concerted cultivation homes. Parents used language to give directions; children were expected to follow and carry out the directions without argument. So profound was this expectation that Lareau and her colleagues noted only one argument between a child and the family during their entire research time with working-class and poor families. This exchange, however, was different from those recorded for concerted cultivation families. Throughout the extended discussion, the child did not contradict the adult's position, but rather simply and quietly stated his preference for a particular kind of food. As such, even when arguments do occur in accomplishment of natural growth homes, their tenor and organization are different from the negotiations and unwillingness to follow directions recorded in concerted cultivation homes.

The consequences of this distinct use of language pattern were many. Harold, like other children being raised in accomplishment of natural growth, rarely "talked back" to his mother or other adult authority figures, nor did he ask his mother to buy him things when out at a store. Lareau observes that a significant distinction of children living in accomplishment of natural growth homes is that they do not develop the language or conversational skills that accrue to middle-class children. For example, Harold's ease with his siblings and peers was palpable, and yet these skills, according to Lareau, "are rendered nearly invisible in the 'real world' of social institutions" (Lareau 2003: 140). She continues, "Educators, health-care professionals, employers, and others accept (and help to reproduce) an ideology that values, among other things, reasoning and negotiating skills, large vocabularies, facility in speaking and working with strangers, and time management the very attributes children [from concerted cultivation] develop in their daily lives" (Lareau 2003: 140). Harold, on the other hand, has close relationships with his extended family, takes directions, structures his own time, and shares language freely with his peers and siblings, yet his access to the linguistic skills that would empower him in institutional settings is absent, in part because of the way in which language is utilized in his family.

Indeed, Lareau documents the more frequent use of physical punishment and physicality more generally to solve and manifest disputes, particularly when compared to homes of concerted cultivation. Lareau also notes that accomplishment of natural growth homes were characterized by greater physical affection as well, observing that hugs, friendly punches in the arms, and wrestling each other in playful ways were far more common here than in concerted cultivation.

The most overarching outcome for this parenting logic is the sense of constraint that is present in adults and becomes part of children's repertoire. In part because of their use of physical punishment, working-class and poor families "display caution and at times mistrust towards individuals in positions of authority and dominant institutions" (Lareau 2003: 157). This sense of caution, coupled with a lack advocacy for one's needs, works to construct a sense of constraint among this population, one that is particularly present in schools. Parents oriented to the logic of accomplishment of natural growth see schools and teachers as responsible for education, and themselves responsible for other important child-care duties. There is, however, an interesting paradox here. While there is substantial mistrust of authority figures among accomplishment of natural growth parents, there is an odd corresponding sense of belief that teachers have authority over a child's education. Parents from accomplishment of natural growth see these professionals as having information that they as parents don't have, and thus teachers are responsible for particular elements of children's lives, while they as parents are responsible for other parts. Compared to concerted cultivation parents, Lareau observes that this distinction "can yield unequal profits to the individuals involved during a historical moment when professionals define appropriate parenting as involving assertiveness and reject passivity as inappropriate" (Lareau 2003: 158). Thus, the long-term outcomes of such a parenting strategy afford accomplishment of natural growth children considerable barriers to self-advocacy, especially when compared to their concerted cultivation counterparts.

While it may seem that there are mounting disadvantages to being raised in an accomplishment of natural growth home, Lareau (2003) is quick to point out that there are also considerable advantages to this orientation. Besides being more compliant, less whiny children, Lareau notes that children in accomplishment of natural growth homes were much nicer to their siblings and extended family, compared to interactions between children in concerted cultivation homes, largely because they had more substantial relationships with them. Additionally, children in accomplishment of natural growth homes have more autonomy and are more practiced at making decisions about their time than those in concerted cultivation. Lareau (2003) concludes, however, that these advantages are not capitalized upon in conventional settings oriented toward the parenting outcomes of concerted cultivation. In these situations, evidence of "good parenting" signaled through extensive cocurricular experiences, experience taking direction from supervising adults, capacity using language for purposes of negotiation, and confidence in interactions with authority figures—is revered. Thus, while the accomplishment of natural growth children have useful skills and qualities, these skills are infrequently noted by schools and health-care systems as advantages. As Lareau (2003) contends,

> one can argue that raising children who are polite and respectful and do not whine, needle or badger their parents is a highly laudable child-rearing goal. Deep and abiding ties with kinship groups are also, one might further argue, important. Rather it is the specific ways that institutions function that end up conveying advantages to middle-class children. In their standards, these institutions also permit, and even demand, active parent involvement [consistent with the parenting logic of concerted cultivation]. (160)

Indeed, as we will see in the next chapter, school expectations overlap significantly with the kinds of skills and corporeal self-control fostered in concerted cultivation homes. By doing so, in a largely unconscious manner, schools amplify middle-class children's home advantage and nullify many of the possible advantages that working-class and poor children might bring with them to school.

Acqusition of (whose?) habitus in the classroom: corporeal advantage at school

Bourdieu's theory holds that the social field children experience shifts dramatically when they begin attending school. Rather than being primarily a member of a small family unit, children in school are now part of a larger, socially heterogeneous groups. In starting school, children become immersed in a new social field that has its own unique rules. Early functional sociologists such as Robert Dreeben (1968) claim that the rules of "doing school" are organized to pass on "essential" social values including "independence, universalism and specificity" (Bain 1985: 146). In explaining Dreeben's position, Bain (1985) explains, "children...learn to accept that in public life, in contrast to family life, one is treated by others as a member of a category (universalism) and that the scope of one person's interest in another is confined to a narrow range specific to the purpose of the interaction (specificity)" (146). Such are the values that underscore adult interactions in public, social circumstances such as school. These values are seen as essential because they form the basis for maintaining macro-social life outside the family setting. As such, these rules appear neutral, "best," or simply "the right way to be in public." When a child anticipates when and how to be independent, and employs universalism and specificity in social situations, he/she demonstrates himself/herself as having self-control. According to Bourdieu, the capacity to anticipate expectations in a field and act accordingly leads individuals to develop a feeling of belongingness, and also leads others to view these individuals as having self-control. As such, having a "feel for the game" is a considerable advantage when learning the hidden curricular expectations of schooling.

While these values may seem neutral and naturally "good," they are in fact applied attributions. The logic behind them betrays a set of beliefs and orientations about what a self-controlled person does, how a self-controlled person speaks, how a self-controlled person conducts himself/herself, etc., which are class-based, and thus are anything but "neutral" or natural. Children who come to school already being familiar with these expectations bring with them a sense of internal knowledge and familiarity of this new social field; children who are less familiar with these implicit notions have more to learn about navigating school corporeal norms. Not only do children growing up in accomplishment of natural growth homes have more to learn due to the difference between their social field and that of the school, but they also may learn that some of their ways of doing things are considered inappropriate by school standards. For instance, schools typically adopt a "use your words" philosophy for solving disputes between children and put a high premium on linguistic competence in negotiating positions. Indeed, many schools in the early grades go so far as to maintain a "hands to yourself" position that is meant to limit physical interaction in favor of verbal arbitration. Such explicit and implicit rules can convey to children who are products of the accomplishment of natural growth that their means of expressing themselves, which relies more heavily on the body than do the expressive practices of children in concerted cultivation homes, are inappropriate for the school setting. For children reared in concerted cultivation homes, such rules reinforce their understanding that the systems they use for solving disagreements are valued and proper.

There are very little existing data exploring the application of these two parenting schemas in school settings. One important study by Nelson and Schutz (2007) documents life at two day-care centers utilizing Lareau's finding of concerted cultivation and accomplishment of natural growth. Profiling two centers that represent each of the parenting positions, Nelson and Schutz (2007) describe the differences in what "quality" day-care means in these differential settings. Central to their findings are the outcomes for the uses of language. At the center serving the professional middle-class population, there is a premium put on "using your words" to solve disputes and explain one's position. Indeed the teachers themselves use language far more than their bodies as a means of communication. As Nelson and Schutz (2007) maintain,

> teachers [working with middle-class children] actively encourage the development of skills that will prepare the children for school success. [These teachers] consistently tell children that they should "use words" to resolve disputes and to express their needs and desires, and they invite children to explain the reasoning for their actions and feelings. They also use a lot of words themselves: they offer full explanations of what they are doing; they help children understand their feelings and the consequences of their actions; and they read books to the children. (13)

Further clouding the notion of neutrality in school rules and systems is the explicit suggestion that schooling is primarily focused on nurturing and developing the mind rather than the body, and that the body's main requirement is to become as neutral a force as possible so as to afford open access to a ready mind. Certainly, the more recent turn toward standardized testing sends an explicit message that it is the cognition of young children that is most important during the school days. And yet, much of the hidden curriculum of early elementary schooling has a great deal to do with the body. By not acknowledging the ways in which school rules are aimed at constructing passive, obedient bodies, teachers can hide behind the rhetoric of "cognitive growth" to maintain controlling, sometimes manipulative stances relative to children's bodies.

If we take as given that schooling is not a neutral process or set of practices, and if we also assume that Lareau's research sheds significant light on how social class influences child-rearing practices, then we can reasonably assume that children will come to school with varying levels of familiarity with school-based corporeal expectations. From Lareau's analysis, we can ask important questions about the consequences of concerted cultivation and the corresponding empowerment that results for children raised in this manner. The familiarity of looking authorities in the eye, shaking hands, having questions at the ready, in essence, presenting oneself as an adult-in-the-making, all weave together to compose a consistent picture of advantage in the social field of school. Because school teachers are primarily middle-class adults, their likely expectations of children correspond more with the logic of concerted cultivation than accomplishment of natural growth (Henry 2013). The ever-increasing stakes of education and teacher evaluation practices linked to student achievement foster a system where teachers are likely to focus their attention on those students who they feel most able to help, namely the students who present like themselves as skilled in the ways of school, and for whom the expectations of school are familiar. Such practices reinforce the unearned advantage that concerted cultivation children experience. In a compulsory schooling regime, sociologists of the body and education researchers should be especially interested in the ways in which children's embodied social class status operates in the school situation. In a time of unprecedented social stratification, many point to schools as sites where children could gain access to the cultural and social capital necessary for social mobility. However, by teaching children to "do school" in only one way—sit straight with feet on the floor, look at the teacher, nod in agreement when the teacher is talking—one might reasonably ask: are schools and teachers complicit in perpetuating an embodied system of social reproduction?

Notes

1 Readers interested in a full explanation for the history of the body in early sociological thought should consult Shilling (2003, chapter two), which has a detailed account of the body in sociology.
2 It is important to note, however, that attentiveness is not a neutral term, but rather one with historically gendered, classed, and raced expectations (Perry, Turner, and Sterk 1992).
3 Bourdieu notes that this discipline is at times instituted from outside the individual in forceful ways in his reference to French schooling, which deliberately attempted to reconstruct the lower classes through their use of particular verbal language, nonverbal communication, and their relationship to time. "It is therefore no accident that a school system which, like the French Ecole Republicaine, was conceived during the Revolution and fully established during the Third Republic, tries to shape completely the habitus of the lower classes, and is organized around the inculcation of a certain relation to language (with the abolition of regional languages, etc.), a relation to the body (disciplines of hygiene, consumption, sobriety - etc.) and a relation to time (calculating - economical - saving, etc)" (Bourdieu 1991: 264).

4
Corporeal Implications of Contemporary Schooling Practices

> **Abstract:** *Lacking empirical data on how teachers read students' bodies for social class status, this chapter suggests that one can consider this question by examining the corporeal implications of contemporary curricular and programmatic influences in schools. This chapter analyzes Ruby Payne's* A Framework for Understanding Poverty *and the Knowledge is Power Program (KIPP) charter school movement as two examples of such educational practices. This chapter argues that due to their deficit constructions of poor children, these programs narrowly define self-control as requiring poor children to comport themselves as middle-class children do, which results in a form of symbolic violence against working-class children.*

> **Keywords:** corporeal practices; neoliberal education; symbolic violence

Henry, Sue Ellen. *Children's Bodies in Schools: Corporeal Performances of Social Class.* New York, Palgrave Macmillan, 2014. DOI: 10.1057/9781137442635.0007.

Given the extensive data for how schools replicate existing social inequalities (as opposed to interrupting them), researchers and educators interested in the workings of social class would be well advised to incorporate the co-constitutive, post-structuralist view, discussed in Chapter 2, into their work. Working from this point of view foregrounds social class and its influence on children's bodies through its focus on the notion of self-control and highlights the importance of seeing children as agentic forces. Altering these basic assumptions about children's agency and the fostering of self-control requires asking questions about the schooling environment and embodiment that do not emerge from traditional views of schooling or the body. Several possible questions result from taking a co-constitutive orientation relative to social class: How do children of different social class status experience their schools corporeally? How does student agency shape middle-class schooling expectations? How do teachers "read" the bodies of children of different social class backgrounds? What are some of the instructional consequences of these (mis)interpretations by educators?

While empirical data are limited, one way to approach these questions theoretically is to examine the overt instruction teachers have received regarding the influence of social class on their students, and to consider the consequences for the overt and hidden curriculum that emerges from such inputs. In this chapter, I review Ruby Payne's (2005) *A Framework for Understanding Poverty*, as one example of a widely used curriculum focused on helping teachers teach poor children. After a brief review of this curriculum, I theorize on the embedded corporeal assumptions about poor children present in the materials, analyze the implications of this broadly used "framework," and consider how children might experience a classroom setting using this approach, focusing specifically on the significant outcomes for self-control that arise. I conduct a similar analysis of the Knowledge Is Power Program (KIPP) charter school approach to education, as another example of an ever-growing method of schooling in the United States. Together these two movements provide powerful examples of the consequences of applying a neoliberal framework in an educational context. These examples illustrate the importance of incorporating notions of self-control and what counts as self-control, into our understanding of how social reproduction happens in schools. My goal is to illustrate the ways in which capitalistic notions of self-control have become embedded in the way personal success is defined and in the explanation of poor children's lack of school success.

The corporeal consequences of a deficit model

In 1996, educational entrepreneur Ruby Payne published the first edition of *A Framework for Understanding Poverty*. Since then, she has built an educational corporation that offers books, professional development training sessions, and other products that claim to help teachers better understand the lives of students living in poverty so that they can teach them better. Her core text has become widely popular; the most recent 4th edition, released in 2005, proclaims to have sold of over one million copies. Payne and her staff offer teachers and public employees in-service presentations throughout the United States, Australia, and Canada. As of 2008, 38 states had adopted Payne's curricula as a central component of school district professional development offerings, among them suburban districts and Native American tribal schools. Many urban districts also use the curricula as a core part of their teacher training (Bomer, Dworin, May, and Semingson 2008). As of October, 2013, Payne's corporation began offering distance education in-service sessions as well.

Several interesting critiques have been made of Payne's work (Gorski 2006; Ng and Rury 2006), the most powerful of which is Bomer et al. (2008) who identify 607 "truth claims" (both explicit and implicit) throughout Payne's text, categorize them into 23 codes, and then analyze whether social science data support such assertions. Their analysis suggests that Payne's work is based upon her own informal impressions gathered during her marriage to a man who grew up in "situational" (temporary) poverty, but for a time lived with family members in "generational" (long-term) poverty, as well as her six years as an elementary principal in an affluent district in Illinois (Payne 2005: 1). This research affirms the work of other critics, namely that the "framework" operates from a deficit model, reifying stereotypes about people in poverty and their children in ways that are deeply troubling. Two of Payne's "truth claims" have deep consequences for the body, largely based in exaggerations of "fact" or outright misinterpretations of data.

Poor bodies are addicted and deficient

Throughout her materials, Payne paints a picture of poor homes as chaotic, out of order spaces. Central to this lack of order is the embedded drug use that Payne asserts is endemic to low-income homes. In her supplemental text, *Bridges Out of Poverty*, Payne asserts that "fifteen to twenty percent of people living in poverty are thought to have substance-abuse issues" (Payne, DeVol, and Smith 2006: 191). Though Payne does not cite her source for this claim, a 2004 report from the National Poverty Center suggests that this estimate may be overstated. This report maintains that substance abuse is just one among many critical features working to keep poor people poor, and that "due to differing definitions and data sources, published prevalence estimates of [drug] use vary widely, from 6.6 to 37 percent of those receiving public aid" (National Poverty Center 2004: 2).

Despite the dubious origins of Payne's estimates, one of the dominant views of the body to come out of such assertions is that parents and caregivers of poor children live in addicted bodies: bodies that violate norms for self-control and discipline. Much like the "overweight" bodies discussed in Chapter 2, bodies that are dependent on drugs are viewed as weak and lazy. Rather than seeing addiction as an occurrence precipitated by poverty, Payne's view is that addiction, caused by a lack of self-control, creates poverty. As part of professional development for teachers, such logic leads teachers to view those marginalized by poverty as responsible for their own impoverished circumstance. The implicit reasoning here leads to the attribution of other moral violations and consequences, such as those articulated by Valencia (1997): "These deficits are evident, according to those holding this view, in limited intellectual abilities, linguistic shortcomings, lack of motivation to learn, and immoral behavior" (Valencia 1997 cited in Bomer et al. 2008: 2529).

Following from this "blame the victim" orientation is the more general notion that poor bodies are naturally deficient. While Payne does not suggest that children come to school with drug-addicted bodies, even a cursory review of her texts indicates that she anticipates serious negative corporeal consequences for growing up in homes where so many adults have substance abuse problems. One of the most significant consequences is that children's bodies and minds are deficient, both in knowledge of and capacity to enact the self-control necessary to approximate middle-class cognitive and corporeal expectations. For example, one encompassing "truth claim" (Bomer et al. 2008) Payne makes throughout *A Framework for Understanding Poverty* is that "the culture of poverty does not provide for success in the middle-class because the middle-class to a large extent requires the self-governance of behavior" (Payne 2005: 77). This claim echoes the principle assertion of the book that poor children will only be successful in school if they learn the middle-class rules of school. The same theory, Payne suggests, holds true for life in general. Knowledge of the "hidden rules" of middle-class life (Payne 2005: 3) is essential for success after school.[1] Some of the "hidden rules" of poverty that Payne offers, and how they differ from those in the middle class, are articulated in a chart indicating the possible explanations for corporeal behaviors frequently seen in poor children:

Behavior related to poverty

- ▸ LAUGH WHEN DISCIPLINED: A way to save face in matriarchal poverty.
- ▸ ARGUE LOUDLY WITH THE TEACHER: Poverty is participatory, and the culture has a distrust of authority. See the system as inherently dishonest and unfair.
- ▸ ANGRY RESPONSE: Anger is based on fear. Question what the fear is: loss of face?
- ▸ INAPPROPRIATE OR VULGAR COMMENTS: Reliance on casual register; may not know formal register.
- ▸ PHYSICALLY FIGHT: Necessary to survive in poverty. Only know the language of survival. Do not have language or belief system to use conflict resolution. See themselves as less than a man or woman if they do not fight.
- ▸ HANDS ALWAYS ON SOMEONE ELSE: Poverty has a heavy reliance on nonverbal data and touch.
- ▸ CANNOT FOLLOW DIRECTIONS: Little procedural memory is used in poverty. Sequence is not used or valued. (Payne: 2005: 79)

The main thrust of the book is Payne's direct instruction on how teachers should use middle-class behavioral norms to counter these troublesome trends. As such, there is a corporeal component to each of these "beliefs about poverty," which Payne wants teachers to look out for in their poor students and correct with the appropriate "middle-class" correlate. For instance, in response to the "hands always on someone else" "problem," teachers should "allow [poor students] to draw or doodle. Have them hold their hands behind their back when in line or standing. Give them as much to do with their hands as is possible in a constructive way" (Payne 2005: 79).

Many of the other corporeal interventions suggested by Payne revolve around replacing poor students' proclivity to respond physically with middle-class speech acts. Consistent with the high priority on linguistic facility in concerted cultivation homes (Lareau 2003), Payne (2005) advocates that teachers use written words, produced both by the teachers and the students, to stifle corporeal performances judged unacceptable for school. One example is Payne's (2005) assertion that in poor homes people "talk incessantly: Poverty is very participatory" (80). To counteract this tendency, Payne suggests "have students write all questions and responses on a note card two days a week. Tell students that each gets five comments a day. Build participatory activities into the lesson" (80).

Payne (2005) also builds the case that the lack of ability to plan or use "procedural memory" (79) is a primary impediment to poor students being able to demonstrate middle-class forms of self-control. Such an absence, Payne (2005) claims, leads to "an inclination toward criminal behavior" (90). Because "little procedural memory" (79) is used in poverty situations, poor children cannot follow directions, are "extremely disorganized," and consequently cannot execute planning in ways consistent with school success. She extends this claim, noting that,

> if an individual cannot plan, he/she cannot predict;
> if an individual cannot predict, he/she cannot identify cause and effect;
> if an individual cannot identify cause and effect, he/she cannot identify consequence;
> if an individual cannot identify consequence, he/she cannot control impulsivity. (Payne 2005: 90)

While Payne's foundations for these assertions may be in question, what is clear is that she has established a persuasive program that reinforces stereotypical, stigmatizing beliefs about children from low-income backgrounds. Such beliefs appear to resonate in educators' thinking about students, as well as their corporeal interaction with these children. As Bomer et al. (2008) assert, "reading her book and hearing Payne speak appears to influence the thinking of many teachers, or else one could not account for her popularity" (2529). How this curriculum influences teachers' thinking is important, because data suggest that teachers' beliefs influence their actions and deeply impact the way they teach and understand student learning ("What Matters Most: Teaching for America's Future: Report of the National Commission on Teaching & America's Future: Summary Report" 1996; Nespor 1987). While there is much that is troubling about these depictions of poor students, at the center of our discussion regarding embodiment are two primary critiques, both of which arise from a post-structuralist analysis of Payne's unsubstantiated assertions: (1) poor students' bodies come to school without the prerequisite self-control necessary for school success and (2) the primary way that poor children should demonstrate their self-control is to perform as middle-class children do.

Payne's suggestions might sound reasonable to some. Myriad data suggest that students from middle- and upper-middle-class backgrounds have stronger academic achievement records in school. One explanation for this achievement record is the idea that the hidden curriculum of school mirrors the rules of home for middle- and upper-middle-class children in ways that create seamless movement for them between these two environments. Because educators also tend to be middle class, their expectations for corporeal performance align with children from this social class background and differ from the corporeal performance expectations held by working-class and poor students. Thus, to middle- and upper-middle-class teachers and students, "appropriate" gestures, eye contact, and other corporeal movement seem "natural" and easily become the normative expectations of the classroom environment.

On the other hand, consistent with post-structuralist theorists, it is important to "challenge the assumption that social *equality* can exist in the absence of social and physical *difference*" (Mason 2013: 694). In other words, the "problem" should not be how to get poor children's bodies to behave more like wealthy children's bodies, as Payne asserts, but rather how to capitalize on the corporeal assets that working-class and poor children bring with them to school such that working-class and poor children's agency is illuminated and extended. Drawing on Paulo Freire's legacy, Bomer et al. (2008) agree, "...nowhere in Payne's work is there a suggestion that students might be taught to think about social class and poverty. There is no hint that people ought to be taught to question the structures that oppress them and others like them systematically" (2530). A similar argument can be made about the corporeal expectations of classroom life. Nowhere in Payne's curriculum are children encouraged to question why they use and move their bodies in certain ways. For example, one possible area of inquiry might be how children from different social class backgrounds demonstrate respect for parents and other adults. Do they look their elders in the eye? Do they look down when adults are talking to them? Do they participate in adult conversation or do they stay quieter when adults are talking?

In fact, Payne's curriculum runs on an opposing model, one that endorses particular corporeal performances without any consideration for their possible marginalizing effects, or the potential assets inherent in the systems working-class and poor children have grown accustomed to from the child-rearing practices used in their homes and their applicability at school. For instance, an educator interested in capitalizing on the skills formed in working-class and poor homes might wonder about Lareau's finding that these children are more accustomed to making choices about their time than children in concerted cultivation homes (Lareau 2003). Indeed, this finding runs counter to Payne's assertion that poor children lack executive functioning skills to organize themselves.

"Self-control," from Payne's point of view, equates to "controlling impulsivity" (Payne 2005: 97), a resource that Payne claims is absent in poor homes and results in self-destructive behavior among children. Payne notes (2012) that knowing the "hidden rules" of other class systems builds the human capital of poor children by teaching them explicitly the rules and expectations of systems they are less familiar with. This approach to developing self-control sounds reasonable enough, but its limitations become obvious when viewed in the larger context of the deficit model Payne advocates. Most problematic here is that simply "putting on" the corporeal moves of the middle- and upper-middle-class is just that, an act, and this recasting of working-class and poor students is likely to remain an act because there is no reciprocal commitment to the practice of agency necessary for full assimilation into middle-class life in Payne's curriculum. Indeed, it may be that marshaling self-control from this limited perspective that creates more obedient, docile students, and perhaps even students who learn subject-matter and perform better on standardized tests. But as Lisa Delpit (1988) has articulated, without a foundation that sees the learner as capable and worthy at its outset, education arranged from this point of view is exchanging one form of oppression (hidden rules) for another (hidden rules exposed that cannot be negotiated or altered with agency).

Looking further into this curriculum, it can be argued that middle- and upper-class children are rewarded for the sorts of self-advocacy skills that enhance their verbal and corporeal agency and that the curriculum works to preserve their already distinct, unearned advantage in the classroom. Such is the outcome of concerted cultivation for middle- and upper-middle-class children, according to Lareau. Indeed, it is this sort of agency—seeing oneself as a critical actor in one's life—that ought to be the point of developing self-control. If, as Payne would have it, the point of developing self-control is to extend a child's obedience and capacity to take direction, then this form of self-control is arguably incomplete.

In addition to the widespread use of Ruby Payne's curriculum, another trend in public schooling is the charter school movement. Several charter school corporations have recently become significant features of the movement, especially in large cities where public school systems have been taken over by the state due to their failure to meet performance standards. One such example is the Knowledge is Power Program, or KIPP, a charter corporation started in 1994 by two former Teach for America teachers. In the next section, I summarize some of the background history of KIPP, as well as the dominant pedagogy and classroom management practices common to these schools. This summary provides a starting point for considering the implications of these core practices for the concept of self-control. What becomes clear from this analysis is that the rhetoric of KIPP, consistent with that of Ruby Payne, exhorts poor children to adopt the verbal and corporeal practices of their middle- and upper-middle-class counterparts in order to succeed in their singular goal of college attendance. Again, rather than emphasizing the development and practice of informed judgment, KIPP pushes an agenda of strict corporeal adherence to middle-class norms of eye contact, shaking hands as a greeting, and other practices as a means of maximizing the development of one's human capital. In such an agenda, docility becomes synonymous with self-control.

KIPP: a story of corporeal control

The KIPP charter school organization was started as the brainstorm of David Levin and Mike Feinberg, two former Teach for America teachers, largely in reaction to their experiences as teachers and their insights into the conditions that they felt kept them from being truly effective as teachers in high-poverty, historically low-achieving schools. The first KIPP school was opened in Houston, Texas, in 1994 after which the program expanded to New York City in 1995. Since then, with the help of significant corporate support as well as federal "Race to the Top" funds, KIPP has grown to serve over 50,000 students in 141 schools spread among 20 states in the nation (http://www.kipp.org/about-kipp/history).

Of these 141 schools, 47 are elementary schools, 74 are middle schools, and 20 are high schools.

The stated primary goal of the KIPP approach is college preparation. Academic and personal preparation for college matriculation frames all of the corresponding decisions about school practice KIPP claims are central to this mission: longer school days, longer school year, a "no excuses" approach to academic and behavioral performance, use of uniforms, and contractual agreements about performance expectations between parents, students, and the schools. Even the mission statements of the elementary KIPP schools mention enrolling in college as the primary aim (http://www.kippphiladelphia.org/schools/kpea).

This singular aim is one that impressed Abigail and Stephan Thernstrom, the authors of *No Excuses: Closing the Racial Gap in Learning* (2003) and whose writing deeply influenced the founders. KIPP founders Levin and Feinberg quickly adopted the "no excuses" approach to learning, as manifested by Rafe Esquith, a fifth-grade teacher at Hobart Boulevard Elementary School in central Los Angeles, whom they met in 1993 as they were working on their charter school concept (Ellison 2012; Thernstrom 2003;). This "no excuses" logic applies to the intense academic preparation that is characteristic of these schools, as well as the character development approach adopted by the program, founded upon Martin Seligman's work in Positive Psychology (Fleming 2010; Peterson and Seligman 2004).

Seligman's work in Positive Psychology is aimed at creating the character traits of those who are resilient and find happiness in their lives (Peterson and Seligman 2004). As journalist Paul Tough reported in a 2006 *New York Times Magazine* article on KIPP schools, the positive psychology basis for KIPP is "an attempt to construct a science of happiness that focuses on 'non-cognitive abilities like self control, adaptability, patience and openness' as being the key to self-fulfillment and success" (Tough 2006 cited in Ellison 2012: 554). These noncognitive capacities frame the notion of character development that drives the instructional model employed in KIPP schools. This model is meant to help children in poverty acquire new capacities that they currently lack, particularly those that drive success, "zest (energy and enthusiasm), grit (persistence and resilience) and self-control" (Fleming 2010 cited in Ellison 2012: 555; Tough 2012). Coupled with intense academics, these virtues make up the driving force behind the KIPP model.

94   Children's Bodies in Schools

This focus on character building is seen by Levin and Feinberg as the foundation for academic success and overcoming the achievement gap (Ellison 2012: 555). By aligning with Seligman, the founders endorse the idea that these children are poor because they have "learned helplessness"—the psychological state Seligman studied in dogs as part of his research on motivation. Briefly, learned helplessness is a psychological condition exhibited by those who have "learned" that nothing they can do can change their situation, and consequently have given up on their efforts to help themselves. The antidote for this situation is Positive Psychology, which delivers the character traits necessary for overcoming learned helplessness. Moving from learned helplessness to learned optimism affords poor students the chance to "retrain...how to think about the adversities they face by externalizing and disputing their pessimistic internal narratives. Developing these skills of externalization and disputation are seen as the key to changing individual behavior toward more productive activities and the pursuit of authentic happiness" (Ellison 2012: 557).

This psychological framework thus serves as the foundation for the five pillars of the KIPP program : "high expectations, choice and commitment, more time, power to lead, and focus on results" (http://www.kipp.org/our-approach/five-pillars). Through the "power to lead" pillar, local school leaders have autonomy to administer their school program in ways they see fit, including hiring and firing staff, and arranging the school days in ways that meet the challenges of their particular student body; as such, there is no universal pedagogical approach utilized within all 141 KIPP schools. However, because the KIPP relies significantly on hiring Teach for America teachers who, by design, have little to no teacher training preparation, the organization runs an induction program prior to the beginning of each school year. It is at this induction orientation that teachers are trained in the primary instructional management strategy that is ubiquitous to KIPP schools and which holds significant insights into how children's bodies are conceived of in these schools: the "no excuses" approach.

An example of the "no excuses" approach can be found in the classroom management practices used in many KIPP schools and summarized in the acronym SLANT: *Sit* up, *Look* and listen, *Ask* and answer questions, *Nod* to show understanding, *Track* the speaker. According to Ellison (2012), "the method constitutes the backbone of student learning centered around direct instructional practices, timed drills, continuous assessment, and the extensive use of mnemonic devices and inspirational chants" (553). Another variation of SLANT is SPARK: "S for sit or stand up straight; P for pen to paper and place your hands on desk; A for ask and answer questions with a straight...elbow; R for respect at all times; K for keep tracking the speaker" (Carr 2013: 11). Through her yearlong shadowing of KIPP teacher Aiden Kelly at Sci Academy High School, a newly opened KIPP school in New Orleans following Hurricane Katrina, Carr (2013) notes Kelly's preparation for explaining to his new ninth graders the precise corporeal moves critical for success,

> Aiden's first day teaching moved with the precision of a military operation....After the uniform check, breakfast, and morning assembly, the students learned how to SPARK.... Each letter was the subject of its own ten-minute mini-lesson. Even on the first day of school, Sci's teachers tried to connect just about every lesson to college: Scholars should sit in SPARK so blood flows to their brains more easily, speeding up their thoughts and facilitating their path to college. Scholars should be able to transition from "silly" to "serious" with a snap of a finger or the clap of a hand because they do not have a second to waste on their path to college. Scholars should wash their hands before leaving the restroom because otherwise they might get germs, which might make them sick, which might cause them to miss school, which would interrupt their path to college. (Carr 2013: 11–12)

At the base of the KIPP pedagogical approach is competition between children and speed in response (Thernstrom and Thernstrom 2003). Thernstrom and Thernstrom (2003) detail in their observations the multiplication table competitions between students, mathematical games where speed is the key, and ubiquitous posters placed in public view declaring rates of homework completion, with hierarchical rankings of students (59–72). Teachers use this competitive heuristic to shape students' bodies and build their self-control.

In their supportive review of KIPP and the strategies utilized in the schools they visited, Thernstrom and Thernstrom (2003) describe teacher-driven directions for students' bodies that they view as essential to establish strong schools that have the capacity to interrupt the achievement gap between poor and wealthy children. In favor of teacher-imposed order, Thernstrom and Thernstrom (2003) document the externally imposed comportment consistent with the prescribed expectation to teach middle-class values. They cite founder Dave Levin who asserts "we are not afraid to set social norms" (Thernstrom and Thernstrom 2003: 67). They continue to document these middle-class corporeal norms in terms that sound consistent with Lareau's (2003) findings, including a focus on linguistic facility, quiet bodies waiting for direction, handshaking to greet others, and eye contact during conversation. "Students at these schools learn to speak politely to teachers and the principal, as well as strangers. It's another invaluable skill.... we found ourselves shaking the hands of a stream of students who told us their names, looked us in the eye, smiled, and welcomed us to their school....youngsters brought in extra chairs on which we could sit to watch a class. Rafe Esquith has his youngsters write individual thank-you notes to visitors" (Thernstrom and Thernstrom 2003: 68). Continuing, Thernstrom and Thernstrom (2003) note that these skills in interacting with the public are what they consider "self-discipline" and include "learning to dress for success, how to sit in a classroom chair, the importance of looking directly at the person to whom you are talking, and the point of standing when greeting someone" (68).

Another ubiquitous modality at KIPP is the corporate framework on which behavior norms are set and academic rewards are proffered to students. The development of "disciplined work habits" (Thernstrom and Thernstrom 2003: 69) is critical here, and the corporeal performances that demonstrate such habits are obvious, at least to Thernstrom and Thernstrom (2003) and KIPP staff. "In schools with a culture of work, no one is slouching in a seat, staring into space, doodling, eating, whispering to classmates, fixing a friend's hair, wandering around the room, or coming and going in the middle of class" (Thernstrom and Thernstrom 2003: 69). In their aim to become good workers, "KIPPsters" demonstrate other corporeal practices requisite of the workplace: "[they] avoid wasting work time by walking down halls rapidly and quietly in orderly lines, and sitting in their classroom seats immediately. They are taught small habits that make a big difference—like using a finger on their left hand to keep track of their place in a book while the right hand is raised to ask a question. They learn to organize their pencils, notebooks, and assignment sheets..." (Thernstrom and Thernstrom 2003: 70).

At Sci Academy in New Orleans, students are called "scholars" from their first day, and are given direct a instruction on what this terminology conveys for their bodily comportment. According to Carr (2013), "over the course of the [first] day, teachers taught mini-classes not only in bathroom protocol and the meaning of SPARK or SPARKing, but how to greet someone (shaking hands firmly while looking the other person in the eye), voice volumes considered appropriate at the school (level 0

= silence, level 1 = whisper, level 2 = quiet talk, level 3 = scholarly voice), and the importance of saying thank you (it shows respect and enthusiasm)" (Carr 2013: 74). In addition, another acronym, NO-DAH, served as a mnemonic for "no desk, arm or hand," as in "Do not rest your head on your desk, arm or hand during class" (Carr 2013: 75).

Among a host of student conduct rules, failure to comport oneself to these corporeal expectations renders a student a "social isolate" (Thernstrom and Thernstrom 2003: 57). At one of the schools they visited, Thernstrom and Thernstrom (2003) learned that students who disobey the code of conduct are sent "to the porch," which at this school meant that while they attend classes, "they wear their KIPP shirts inside out and cannot talk to or eat with their classmates" (Thernstrom and Thernstrom 2003: 57). At Sci Academy, students isolated for violations of the school's six values—"responsibility, perseverance, integrity, empathy, courage, and community"—were separated from peers at lunch and used tape to cover the KIPP emblem on their uniforms to signal their "temporary estrangement" (Carr 2013: 24).

Beyond social isolation, failure and success in meeting these corporeal and academic expectations is met with another habit of the workplace: financial compensation. All the KIPP schools Thernstrom and Thernstrom (2003) visited had some form of "token economy" where students who abided by school rules were rewarded with KIPP dollars to spend in the school store, and were paid a regular "wage" in addition to earning bonus dollars for obtaining a perfect test score, maintaining perfect attendance, and the like. Similarly, fines are meted out for failing to maintain an organized desk, being tardy, or violating other school and classroom rules. Esquith, the fifth-grade teacher in central Los Angeles, goes a step further in his classroom, assigning a monetary value to various student seats in the room and charging students "rent" to occupy their seat, which is drawn from their wage. As Thernstrom and Thernstrom (2003) describe in detail: "[the students pay rent], but if they have earned and saved enough, they can buy their seat as a condo.... they can buy other students' seats, at which point rent is paid to them. (The kids know that if they are profligate and can't pay rent, they could be 'homeless' and find themselves sitting on the floor, although we saw everyone safely in their chairs)" (73).

Some describe this style of teaching and learning as "traditional" and maintain that the conditions in which poor and racial minority children live call for the imposition of structure and order, the components of success that are missing from their home lives (Thernstrom and Thernstrom 2003). Such constructions are consistent with Payne's view of poor children's homes as chaotic, unstructured locales. Others suggest that these approaches, contrary to their stated mission and purpose, represent the very social reproduction practices that confirm the place of working class, poor, and racial minorities at the bottom of the social mobility ladder (Horn 2010; Ellison 2012). Andre Perry, an associate director at Loyola University's Institute for Quality and Equity in Education, suggests that KIPP represents a "lockdown" movement that rose to popularity in the 1980s and 1990s, when some educators responded to high crime and murder rates by instituting zero-tolerance school disciplinary policies and other "lockdown" approaches to schooling. "We've never come out of [lockdown]," Perry maintains (Carr 2013: 81). Perry continues his critique by noting the troubling overlap between schools where these policies remain intact and those with high concentrations of poor students and students of color. "Perry is troubled by the idea that children—and poor children of color most especially—need to be controlled. 'There's an insidious mistrust of children reflected in having them walk on lines or making them stay silent'" (Carr 2013: 81).

On the one hand, there is an apparent overlap between KIPP's firm disciplinary approach and strict adherence to corporeal expectations and the disciplinary style of working-class and poor families documented in Lareau's work (Lareau 2003). Indeed, Carr (2013) observes that many poor parents support KIPP's strict approach, often calling for even more firmness and direction (94). As Carr (2013) notes, other studies have also documented how different parenting styles and preferences correlate to parents of different social class backgrounds, with low-income families tending toward authoritarian parenting styles, characterized by insisting on compliance, silence, and spanking and hitting children in order to protect them from external threats such as drugs, racist interactions, and other adult crimes (Burgess and Brown 1999; Sherman and Harris 2012).

On the other hand, it is reasonable to raise the question of whether this approach to discipline is successful in creating the academic and social achievement in schools more commonly experienced by children raised in concerted cultivation homes. The data that have been gathered are spotty, but even among the various types of studies that have been conducted on KIPP and its outcomes, the sole assessments have been results on state and national standardized tests in reading and math. Not queried are the outcomes for students' self-control or the cultivation of a sense of internal capacity for students to create the lives they wish to have. Indeed, much of the criticism of the Positive Psychology movement stems from the notion that rather than inculcating personal qualities of endurance and resilience that can help people to remain dedicated to goals in the face of disillusionment, Positive Psychology's individualistic emphasis keeps individuals from seeing structures around them and seeking to change those that might actually affect life outcomes. One likely psychological outcome of this orientation is the construction of individuals who see themselves as solely responsible for all elements of failure and less able to see how factors outside of their control may have impeded their progress, resulting in a sense of unnecessary personal defeat (Ellison 2012). Such were the findings of MacLeod's (2008) ethnography of social reproduction in the schooling of two groups of boys in inner city Chicago. One group, the Brothers, played by the rules of school and had internalized the achievement ideology of school: do what you are told, achieve good grades, and success will result. When these boys were not able to alter their cultural capital to achieve success after high school, they saw their defeat as solely their own and were unable to see how their schooling experience had factored into their restricted future opportunities.

Also problematic is that practices used for disciplining the body in the KIPP approach to corporeal performance construct subjugated physical selves through instructional techniques that create dependency on the teacher to structure the course and nature of daily activity. In a turn on Seligman's construct of "learned helplessness," Horn (2011) uses the same term to describe the constructed dependence students develop for their teachers' directions, which he claims "[subtly shapes and produces] individuals that are economically productive and politically docile" (Horn cited in Ellison 2012: 570). KIPP's disciplinary tactics require unquestioning recognition of teacher authority, seeking to equate "self-control" and a "good" body with a compliant body. As Ellison (2012) maintains, one reasonable conclusion of the KIPP approach is that

> [c]lassroom activities force students to engage in patterned behaviors designed with the specific pedagogical intent of teacher-centric rote learning and to engage in scripted chants and songs in which the movements of students' bodies [are] both prescribed and monitored for compliance. Indeed, these patterned behaviors are among the first lessons that KIPP students

learn in their first summer school session, and these behaviors play out in a choreographed sequence of content delivery, drills, and assessment oriented around a specific timeline defined by state assessment regimes. (570)

A major problem here, similar to that associated with Ruby Payne's approach, is that while the corporeal practices employed at KIPP resemble the physical moves of families using the logic of concerted cultivation, these embodiments are unlikely to construct the type of agency that children of concerted cultivation experience. When children enroll at KIPP, they learn early on that corporeal performances they may have used at home are not valuable in this school setting, requiring instead the installation of a middle-class corporeal regime that is to be practiced to the level judged valuable by the external authority of the teacher. Marquisha Williams, a new student to Sci Academy in 2008, recalls her first day receiving this message loud and clear: "[This was] academic boot camp where they said, 'These are the rules. They are not changing. Follow them'" (Carr 2013: 75). Again, Carr (2013) quotes Andre Perry on the disconnect between the middle-class corporeal expectations of KIPP and the experience of agency that undergirds these same corporeal performances when enacted by middle-class people: "I don't think a lot of poor parents really understand the freedoms associated with a middle-class lifestyle...some of them 'feel that intense structure and rules are what their children need to achieve because that's all they know'" (Carr 2013: 104). Indeed, this reliance on strict rules and "no excuses" rhetoric may come especially easy in a system that (1) sees students as deficient in "natural" qualities of success and (2) does not incorporate agency of students in its school program. Agency seems to be a missing piece of the KIPP equation.

While activating the sheer physical expectations of concerted cultivation, the KIPP approach overlooks the other important variables of concerted cultivation, namely the use of judgment and negotiation that helps to foster children who believe themselves powerful in making decisions. Children raised in the accomplishment of natural growth actually have a good deal of experience making decisions for themselves in their homes. But the use of this judgment-making experience as a form of agency in one's own life is different than the type of binary, "follow the rules or leave the school," sort of judgment practiced in the KIPP environment. KIPP maintains that because of the second pillar of "choice," children and parents who do not wish to follow these expectations can practice their agency by choosing to leave the school. But this is a narrow form of agency, certainly inconsistent with the notions outlined in Chapter 2 by Carrie Noland (2010), whereby practices performed by individuals *change the situation* in situ, or the type that is readily evident in Lareau's data where concerted cultivation children are able to argue and negotiate for power within their family system.

Further, for KIPP students, the range within which to demonstrate the capacity for self-control in school, which by all accounts means complete compliance with school code, is very limited. Indeed, this is the deal that KIPP makes with students and parents: follow our rules and we will set you up for college matriculation and success. Unfortunately, because this definition of self-control requires students to comport their bodies in middle-class ways without the corresponding cognitive and corporeal opportunities for agency over the lives they live in school, these students are more likely to perform physical docility in school without the accompanying self-advocacy that emerges from the type of agency practices in middle-class homes (Lareau 2003) and schools (Calarco 2011; Nelson and Schutz 2007). Alison Drake, a KIPP teacher in New Orleans, references this missing quality for Geraldlynn, a former student preparing for college:

> the teen's greatest challenge in college will probably be self-advocacy. "It's important for our kids who go off to an environment where they don't have a lot of experience to be able to advocate for themselves," her teachers says. "...Geraldlynn works really hard, but she's never been the kid with the highest skills. She doesn't have the ability to breeze through schoolwork, and if, in a college class, she doesn't know what a professor is saying she's going to have to have the confidence to raise her hand or go see them later." (Carr 2013: 26)

As such, KIPP's focus on controlling the bodily comportment of its students to the detriment of their agency underscores its foundational belief that the bodies and corporeal gestures of its students are major impediments to their future success. The narrowness of this belief is one of the major criticisms of KIPP, one that arises from KIPP's prescription of the Protestant Work Ethic and which also serves as the moral foundation for finding fault in those with nonnormative bodies. The message of KIPP is that "hard work is a reflection of moral excellence and invariably leads to success" (Lack 2009, quoted in Ellison 2012: 563). A significant component of demonstrating hard work in the KIPP context is coordinating one's body to the corporeal expectations of KIPP. At KIPP, physical comportment is a proxy for self-control. Because these rules are ubiquitous throughout the school setting, knowing these rules and expectations likely helps children anticipate their future and determine what will come next as a result of their choices. But is this self-control in the most authentic sense? Certainly following school rules is not necessarily a bad capacity, but to equate self-control with obedience is to minimize the fullest definition of the term. The Protestant Work Ethic principle underlying these rules reinforces the notion that if children are successful, it is because of their own positive attitude and effort. Concomitantly, failure is also individual; lack of success indicates that the child did not try hard enough and is solely responsible for his/her own outcomes.

Compulsory docility: what passes for "self-control"

One need not look only at the rigid, militaristic approach to education that KIPP represents or the stereotypical beliefs foundational to Ruby Payne's curriculum to find examples of narrow and class-based views of self-control in schools. Researcher Megan Watkins takes up the importance of developing self-control and the concomitant role of the body in her qualitative analysis of elementary school children learning to write (Watkins 2012). While conducting observations in six classrooms in two primary schools in Australia, Watkins (2012) documents the different corporeal expectations teachers held that correspond with their educational philosophy. Noting that children in one school were much more skilled at learning to write—both actual handwriting and generating text—Watkins (2012) suggests that while "many children enter school already predisposed to write," they must still be trained through an apprenticeship approach to write *as adults do*, which to Watkins means developing the kind of self-control that adults exhibit (26). Thus, Watkins defines self-control as imitation of adult corporeal performance.

Watkins (2012) argues that the most efficient way to encourage this form of corporeal self-control is through teacher-driven instruction that shapes student practice into adult practice. In what now appears a familiar refrain pulled from the logic of concerted cultivation, as Watkins elaborates, her class-based bias for certain kinds of bodily performances emerges: "What [natural learners] possess may appear as natural due to its habituation, but what they have acquired prior to entering school is a particular habitus for learning. They are comfortable sitting at a desk and have considerable bodily control when completing work. The ease and early success experienced by many children who have attended childcare...can be partly attributed to this bodily preparedness for the classroom" (Watkins 2012: 26–27). She articulates in her conclusion why the students at the more affluent school were better writers:

> the students at Northside were not only better writers because of their class background, or a complementarity between the language and values of their home and school....[They] were better writers...largely because of the capacitating properties of their teachers' pedagogy....[Student success] was dependent upon disciplinary techniques that invested...students' bodies with a capacity for sustained application and the knowledge and skills upon which effective literate practice is based....[Their] teachers' pedagogical approach [was] characterised by a considerable degree of teacher-directedness and a form of classroom management that was designed to instil a scholarly docility in students. (Watkins 2012: 196–197)

Watkins contrasts this teacher-led approach to the more psychological philosophy invested in Westville, where teachers aimed to make school a comfortable, supportive environment, and by consequence, did not make as many corporeal demands on children during instruction. As Watkins writes, "[at Westville] the pedagogic regime...exerted very little disciplinary force upon [students'] bodies leaving them largely reliant on the dispositions formed outside of school....As the students at Westville seemed less amenable to the required corporeality of schooling, the teachers found it difficult to utilise more stringent disciplinary techniques" (Watkins 2012: 197).

Watkins furthers her argument by suggesting that the aim of efficient literacy instruction is ultimately to remove the "problem" of the body from the learning equation, installing instead a bodily form that works as a tool for demonstrating the effort of the mind. Once the teacher has been successful in generating this sort of adult corporeal self-control into children's muscle memory, the sheer biodynamics of producing written text becomes easier: "the body then disappears." (Watkins 2012: 27). Watkins (2012) maintains that having the body "disappear" is a worthy goal because it reflects the "embodiment of scholarly posture that is a necessary precursor to the self-discipline required for independent learning and academic work" (27). "In children whose bodies are accustomed to sitting at a desk and concentrating for sustained periods, their body in a sense disappears as they begin to habituate a scholarly posture... thereby reduc[ing] cognitive load, resulting in a greater capacity for conscious thought" (Watkins 2012: 27). It is easy to imagine many teachers agreeing with such a stance. Any position that offers apparently solid educational philosophy for reducing the movement and gesturing of 20 (or more) young learners in a classroom might seem beneficial.

And yet, despite appearing common sensical, it is reasonable to wonder whether this is the only form of corporeal self-control useful for schooling. Among other approaches that can be contrasted with Payne, KIPP, and Watkins' points of view are the Doctrine of Liberty promoted by Maria Montessori[2] and the varieties of self-control practiced in Japanese elementary schools documented by Catherine Lewis in *Educating Hearts and Minds* (1995). Both of these educational practices are lodged in the progressive education movement of the 20th century, which have at their core John Dewey's central principle that schools should develop and extend the practice of individual liberty: the heart of democracy.

A different view of self-control: Montessori and Japanese elementary education

Much has been written about Maria Montessori and the educational principles she put in place in Casa dei Bambini. Central to Montessori's philosophy is the cultivation of self-control in children, or what she called "the practice of liberty," through self-directed experimentation in the classroom. What looks like mere "play" to many in an American audience is exactly the kind of "work" (Thayer-Bacon 2012: 12) that children must engage in to develop their internal capacity for liberty. Thayer-Bacon (2012) describes Montessori's approach: "allowing children to choose what they are interested in as an activity, the children will take care of their deep-seeded needs for independence and self-control, as well as other needs such as order and silence, and will learn how to monitor their own behavior through what she labeled as their 'work'" (12). After intense observations of young learners, including those living in poverty, Montessori concluded that all children can "develop a strong ability to concentrate their minds and control their bodies if given the chance to do so" (Thayer-Bacon 2012: 12). In her comprehensive biography of Montessori, Kramer (1988) offers a list of now familiar conventions of progressive early childhood education that have their roots in Montessori's theory, including:

- the idea that children should be free to choose their own work and follow their interests and work at their own pace,...
- the idea that the child is not just a smaller version of the adult,
- the idea that children take real pleasure in learning and that real learning involves the ability to do things for oneself, [and]
- the idea that children will establish their own order and quiet if given interesting work to do. (Kramer quoted in Thayer-Bacon 2012: 16)

Most important for our purposes in seeing a contrasting type of self-control to the neoliberal approach consistent with Payne, KIPP, and Watkins is Montessori's claim that the role of education and schools is to "help each child develop to his or her full potential" (Thayer-Bacon 2012: 16). A central difference here between the neoliberal approach and Montessori's student-centered orientation stems from different core conceptions of the child, particularly notions of poor children of color. The neoliberal viewpoint advances from the notion that poor students and students of color do not come to school prepared "naturally" for school success, as evidenced by their continuing academic failure relative to their wealthier, white peers. As such, this perspective asks, "what are these learners missing that keeps them from experiencing school success?" In Payne, KIPP, and Watkins, the answer to this question is, in part, that children lack self-control which is demonstrated by their lack of corporeal control. All three approaches, consequently, are variants on the deficiency theme.

Payne (2005) suggests that because poor children grow up in chaotic, drug-addicted homes, they tend toward impulsivity. KIPP asserts that poor children lack corporeal structure central to school success, hence its rigid control of students' bodies with uniforms, group chants, and detailed corporeal classroom management strategies. Watkins (2012) contends that students' failure in learning to write can be traced to inexperience with "scholarly docility" (197) and some teachers' unwillingness to assert authority requiring students to sit in desks for long periods and maintain a mostly silent workspace.

Montessori sees the situation differently. Rather than seeing the external imposition of discipline on students' bodies as a primary tool to construct an orderly, learning-filled classroom, Montessori asks, what could students be doing that would afford them the internal experience of corporeal discipline? For Montessori, the development of self-governance is a key element in developing academic competence. But the ability to achieve academic success alone is not, and should not be, the sole determinant of "potential" in a student. The capacity to engage with others, to practice the art of self-control and self-discipline *toward one's own ends* and *chosen achievement* is another necessary component of schooling experience. In essence, Montessori has her vision aimed at cultivating an independent thinker, someone who can observe a social situation and decide how to act and behave in that situation to further his/her own and others' goals. Rather than training a student to simply follow the rules and stay out of trouble, Montessori seeks to educate a child with the power of discernment and an internalized sense of agency.

A similar approach is taken in Japanese elementary classrooms through their application of Deweyan principles. Catherine Lewis' (1995) thorough description of the goals of the Japanese ministry for early childhood education and the ways in which classrooms enact these goals offers a clear picture of putting young children in positions of authority and responsibility, utilizing their thinking and problem-solving skills in the running of the daily functions of the class, and developing a sense of what Lewis (1995) terms "self-management." Lewis (1995) documents how Japanese teachers encouraged children to consider these important ideas throughout the school days in the real situations in which they found themselves. In the development of the 94 unique goals collected from all first-grade classrooms that comprised her qualitative study of 15 classrooms in 13 schools, some goals were selected by faculty, student council, the class, or small groups within the class. All goals were written and posted in these classrooms in the *hiragana* alphabet so that they were readable by the first graders. Of the 94 goals, four themes emerged: friendliness, persistence, energy, and self-management (Lewis 1995: 44).

Related to corporeal expectations, Lewis (1995) observed that "energy, enthusiasm (*genki*)" was expressed by classroom goals focused on helping students to "play energetically" or "be energetic" (Lewis 1995: 49). She goes on to write that during one of her observations, "students ran at full speed around a first-grade classroom" and, when children were sluggish, teachers often remarked that "there's not much *genki* today" (Lewis 1995: 49). Children were expected to "act like children," which in the Japanese setting meant "noisy exuberance" (Lewis 1995: 49). In their famous work *Preschool in Three Cultures,* Tobin, Wu, and Davidson (1991) describe the priority voiced by Japanese early childhood educators that children be "*kodomorashii*" (childlike) and that such protection from examination preparation (common in the middle and high school setting) was necessary to maintain this period of childhood (cited in Lewis 1995: 49).

In addition to physical stamina and expression, Japanese elementary classrooms featured a heavy emphasis on the development of self-management, primarily through regular and important responsibilities children maintained for the classroom. Throughout the classrooms that Lewis (1995) visited, all had multiple charts detailing the structure of the day and the options children had for free time. Charts were also an important mechanism through which children were encouraged to complete their chores for the classroom. Coupled with teacher- and student-led reflection (*hansei*) periods throughout each school day, these features of classroom life reminded children of the important physical duties they had: "had they watered the class garden and fed the animals? Remembered to bring from home all required items? Kept their desks neat? Laid out the correct notebooks and textbooks before each class?" (Lewis 1995: 51). Concomitantly, teachers described the importance of introducing rules and norms "naturally" (*shizen ni*) and "without force" (*muri naku*) (Lewis 1995: 108). Lewis (1995) quotes a preschool teacher commenting on her work in this regard with young learners taking advantage of opportunities that arise naturally in the communal setting of a classroom:

> Every day for the last few months a boy named Ken has closed the classroom door at the end of the school day. Every single day I've said thanks and mentioned to the class that the neighborhood cats would come in if Ken didn't close the door. But so far, the children have not picked up on my hint to add this to the regular chores. But I don't want to tell them.... Children must learn through their own activities. It should come from the children. (Lewis 1995: 109–110)

Such is the nature of the internalization of self-management and self-control in the Japanese elementary system.

The contrast evident in the corporeal expectations of the student-centered approach versus the deficit approach foundation of Payne, KIPP, and Watkins raises an issue critical to our conversation of authentic self-control: how can a teacher balance his/her use of power to cultivate corporeal routine that leads to generative capacities which then afford children the opportunity to use academic skills for their own and communal aims? In other words, what sorts of corporeal performances in the classroom can promote liberty rather than sheer conformity? Is it possible for the abstracted body evident in the Payne, KIPP, and Watkins' approaches to have a full form of self-control evident in the Montessori and Japanese elementary settings? Watkins (2012) argues that students' corporeal practice apprenticing the academic standards and expectations of the teacher represents a means by which to experience their liberty. "Conforming to [a] teachers' desires does not lessen [a student's] pre-existing sense of self; rather it leads to the acquisition of particular dispositions constitutive of her own subjectivity" (Watkins 2012: 22). But how? Watkins clearly outlines an enduring philosophical question: can a teacher "make" a student corporeally perform in a certain manner without the force of her efforts being coercive and undercutting intrinsic self-control? Montessori and Lewis suggest that allowing students' self-governance and incorporating into academic activities work that foregrounds students creating an academic environment that meets their goals can go at least some of the way toward answering this important question.

Future questions about children's bodies in contemporary schooling

At this point in the analysis, numerous queries related to children's bodies arise. Why must there be one "scholarly posture"? Is the disappearance of the body a pedagogical aim for which to strive? Whose bodies are seen as "better" when "disappearance" is the goal? How are those who have more difficulty making their bodies "disappear" evaluated in such a system? What are some long-term consequences of such an abstraction of mind and body for young learners? What conception of self-control does such an approach incur? How does a child's social class status figure into a teacher's assessment of the child's corporeal capacity for self-control?

Addressing some of these questions, well-known early childhood theorist and anthropologist Joseph Tobin argues that the "disappearance" of the body in early childhood education is a deeply troubling trajectory. Tobin (2004) notes six causes for the continued abstraction of children's bodies from their educational experience: the moral panic surrounding preschools as sites of sexual predation; the disciplining of sexuality through academic, medical, and legal lenses; the diminished psychoanalytic influence in early childhood theory; an increased focus on linguistic competence among the very young; the increased reliance on brain-based research for educational decision-making; and the application of phonics instruction in the early grades (promoted by No Child Left Behind legislation). He argues that while it is possible to see these movements as simply a disturbing combination of random factors, in fact, their influence on the body is not an unanticipated by-product shifting political values. "What these six trends have in common is a focus on rationality, control, and risk avoidance. Collectively, they suggest the need for order, policing, discipline, and surveillance" (Tobin 2004: 124). Indeed, Ruby Payne's curriculum, the KIPP approach, and Watkins' research conclusions seem apt examples of the trends Tobin identifies.

The neoliberal underpinning of constrained self-control

Returning to the concept of neoliberalism, it is possible to view the sustained and growing abstraction of children's bodies from their minds as part of the same shift that has influenced politics, economics, business, and education to focus on the presumed benefit of markets, choice, and competition. This neoliberal point of view is characterized by a focus on the individual rather than the social structures and institutions that compose society; the individual is conceived of as a consumer rather than a citizen, and one is valued according to the financial contribution he/she can make to the economy. As Harvey (2007) maintains, neoliberalism is "in the first instance a theory of political economic practices that proposes that human well-being can be best advanced by liberating individual entrepreneurial freedoms and skills within an institutional framework characterized by strong private property rights, free markets and free trade" (2). Central to this neoliberal vision of the individual are perseverance, learned optimism, and self-reliance. In education, children who make the best future consumers are those who demonstrate "grit" and dogged determination (Duckworth and Seligman 2005; Duckworth, Quinn, and Seligman 2009). Grit and determination form the basis for what is described as "self-control" in a neoliberal context, as these are believed to be the characteristics of those who persevere without complaint in the face of adversity.

While no one would be successful in mounting a campaign against perseverance, defining self-control with a "first-principles" appeal narrows the possibilities for children, poor, and wealthy alike, to demonstrate varieties of self-control that fit multiple situations, as well as in ways that fit their family social class dynamics. In the 1960s and 1970s, the social reproduction critique of schools was that tracking and ability grouping, coupled with the achievement ideology, created schools that effectively slotted learners into their future roles in capitalism–either as workers or as bosses. In our current neoliberal educational moment, another dimension of school-based social reproduction practice is added to the picture: constricted notions of corporeal self-control. Such notions and their corporeal applications help sustain stereotypes of poor and working-class children as "needing structure," which both KIPP and Ruby Payne's curriculum play upon for support. Both approaches and their neoliberal bases underscore the further abstraction of children's minds from their bodies and reify the notion that, in order to achieve school success and shrink the academic achievement gap, poor and working-class children will have to assimilate middle- and upper-middle-class norms of corporeal performance.

While it is true that all schooling changes learners, there are arguably some adaptations schools construct that render what Bourdieu maintains is a form of symbolic violence. As Bourdieu (1991) explains, those whose habitus conflicts with dominant schooling corporeal expectations within schools are at great risk of experiencing symbolic violence: a concealed assault on the students' sense of self through consistent messaging that they must change who they are in order to be successful in the school environment justified through the discourse of "best practices" and standardized outcomes. Because of the middle-class habitus that educators typically inhabit, many are unable to understand their insistence on a particular corporeal expectation as a form of symbolic violence:

> The distinctiveness of symbolic domination lies precisely in the fact that it assumes, of those who submit to it, an attitude which challenges the usual dichotomy of freedom and constraint.... *The propensity to reduce the search for causes to a search for responsibilities makes it impossible to see that intimidation, a symbolic violence which is not aware of what it is (to the extent that it implies no act of intimidation) can only be exerted on a person predisposed (in his habitus) to feel it, whereas others will ignore it....* There is every reason to think that the factors which are most influential in the formation of the habitus are transmitted without passing through language and consciousness, but through suggestions inscribed in the most apparently insignificant aspects of the things, situations and practices of everyday life. Thus the modalities of practices, the ways of looking, sitting, standing, keeping silent, or even or speaking ("reproachful looks" or "tones," "disapproving glances" and so on)

are full of injunctions that are powerful and hard to resist precisely because they are silent and insidious, insistent and insinuating. (51)

Applying Bourdieu's critique to children's bodies, symbolic violence in schools occurs when teachers signal that who a student is, at their core, is flawed in such a way that the only antidote is to become someone else. In other words, symbolic violence occurs when educational practices seek to substitute the values and communication systems of the powerful in place of those associated with one's family and community.

Concerns about children's bodies in contemporary schooling are exceptionally salient in the neoliberal era. Significant scholarly work critiques the neoliberal turn in education (Binkley 2011; Kasser, Cohn, Kanner, and Ryan 2007) where the individual becomes preeminent, and the values of self-discipline and self-control become the essential tools one uses to exercise his/her individual rights and develop his/her human capital. Under this ideology, school practices, such as those revealed in Ruby Payne's curriculum and the KIPP program, become powerful disciplining devices, helping to instill notions of self-discipline and the need for personal responsibility that are eventually able to be "govern[ed] at a distance" (Ouellette 2007: 151).[3] When applied in an educational context, neoliberalism turns learners into consumers and entrepreneurs who must develop the characteristics of those who persevere. Indeed, as a way of coping in a competition that unfairly privileges some over others, Positive Psychology and its emphasis on individual characteristics has been used to mask and maintain these systems of inequality. Such use of Positive Psychology has been borrowed from the business world where aims of increasing productivity in employees by "building the psychological capacities... such as hope, optimism, and resilience... 'statelike' qualities that remain consistent over time and that lead to 'self-directed motivating mechanisms" have always been paramount (Youssef and Luthans 2007, quoted in Ellison 2012: 559).

This broader context for neoliberalism creates new challenges for citizens, and presents a significant obstacle for developing the liberty and judgment of poor children in America's schools that utilize Payne's curriculum, the KIPP approach, or teacher-driven pedagogies such as those that Watkins advises. The rhetoric of the neoliberal philosophy rests upon the notion of the liberal self—the self as an agent in his/her own life. This notion of the liberal self has at its base the idea that individuals make the world in which they live. Liberated adults have agency over their own lives. This rhetoric, however, runs counter to the tools and pedagogical practices KIPP utilizes, and those that Payne and Watkins advocate, which foreground teacher-authority over student-authority and narrow "right" ways of using the body built upon artificial and limited ideas about what sorts of corporeal performances lead to learning. Such stances overlook the enormous influence of poverty on children—explored in detail in Chapter 2—and frame the only appropriate unit of analysis as the individual, thereby sustaining the notion that if an individual is unsuccessful in his/her life, the only reasonable explanation is that he/she did not try hard enough or have a positive enough attitude. As Ellison (2012) concludes, this situation likely creates individuals who embrace the status quo despite the claim that comporting oneself in this way will support greater agency in one's own life: "...an important criticism [of Positive Psychology and KIPP]...[is] its focus on a decontextualized *I* in which success and failure are directly related to individual character and the goal is to reconcile, or discipline, individuals to situational dynamics beyond their control" (566).

By pushing these causal beliefs (do as I say and you will be successful; maintain a positive attitude and you will be successful), Ellison (2012) maintains that the link between neoliberal politics and educational practices is made. He observes that KIPP's orientations are "characterized by the social processes of individualization and consumerism commonly associated with the (re)emergence of neo-liberal thought and politics over the past 40 years" (567). Ellison quotes Clarke (2004) in asserting that neoliberal thought has at its core this conflicted relationship with reality–on the one hand asserting a picture of reality and on the other hand trying to construct a notion of reality simultaneously. "Put crudely, neo-liberalism tells stories about the world, the future and how they will develop—and tries to make them come true" (Clarke 2004 quoted in Ellison 2012: 568).

One clear conclusion for "self-control" from this point of view is that it eerily reproduces the cycles of social class segregation it ostensibly seeks to undermine. The rhetoric of education models such as the KIPP, Payne, and Watkins claim to interrupt the achievement gap by teaching poor children what middle-class children already know—that they should be agents in their own lives and that middle-class corporeal norms ensure such agency. And yet, due to the characterization of poor children as deficient and lacking the "structure" needed for success, instilling such middle-class corporeal structures only serves to reinscribe poor children's segregated position within the school, thereby increasing the likelihood of their place in the lower strata after schooling.

Regardless of the rhetoric to the contrary, the kind of self-control instilled by the KIPP process and Payne's curriculum and Watkins' analysis is not the same as that passed from the middle-class parents to their children, largely because they engender a sense of capacity rather than dependence on the external authority of the teacher. This lack of independence occurs when a student's own thinking is thought to be deficient and in need of replacement with the thinking of an external authority. Central to what is absent in the KIPP, Payne, and Watkins portrayals are opportunities for authentic authority and for cultivating intrinsic self-control, characteristic of Montessori and Japanese elementary education.

Through the imposition of unquestioned norms supported by a neoliberal view of the individual, these "cultural-interventionist" schooling practices seek to install an internalized set of capacities to foster a certain view of an individual as an entrepreneurial, freedom-seeking consumer (Shuffelton 2013). This orientation misrepresents "self-control" as obedience and compliance to an external frame of expectations distant from an authentic form that affords individuals the capacity to make decisions for the self with self and others' interests and needs considered. As such, this narrow conception of self-control cultivates an unreflective docility that in the end works to create a highly sustainable and unimpeachable form of social reproduction in schools.

Importantly, as this book has sought to illustrate, contrary to many teachers' regard of the body as a mere obstacle to subsequent good thinking (e.g., "if I can just get these kids to sit still I can teach them!"), there is in fact another way to view students' bodies in the classroom. A detailed focus on corporeality in the classroom asks teachers to consider how they might understand children's bodies as related to their minds. Such a reorientation to the mutuality of the mind/body promises not only to illuminate teacher-held stereotypes about what bodies are most valuable, but also to reveal the covert, ubiquitous practices of the elementary classroom that unconsciously (though powerfully) reinscribe power in those who practice these embodied gestures as a product of their social class upbringing, and subordination in those who do not. Reinstating the place of the body in the classroom, seeing the body as a legitimate partner in learning rather than a set of organs to be wrangled into place before learning can occur, would be one important step toward not only addressing the abstraction of the mind/body, but also foregrounding a more democratic view of the development of "self-control" in elementary classrooms. Asking such questions restores thinking about the power of social class on children's bodies and opens new avenues for theorizing and studying the impact of social class on children's early schooling experiences.

Notes

1 Readers should note that this argument as Payne (2005) makes it is very different from the argument made by Lisa Delpit in *Other Peoples Children*. Delpit does not assume a deficit stance toward diverse learners and, as such, uses the direct teaching of "middle-class" ways of speaking to afford learners additional choices about voice, tone, and language use while supporting the use of their native languages.
2 It is beyond the scope of this book to explore in detail all the important facets of Montessori education. Interested readers would be well advised to review several seminal texts on the subject, including Montessori's (1964) *The Montessori Method* and *The Discovery of the Child* (1948/2004); Gutek's (2004) *The Montessori Method: The Origins of an Educational Innovation: Including an Abridged and Annotated Edition of Maria Montessor's The Montessori Method*; Kramer's (1988) *Maria Montessori: A Biography*; E. M. Standing's (1998) *Maria Montessori: Her Life and Work*; and Wentworth and Wentworth's (2013) *Montessori for the New Millineum: Practical Guidance on the Teaching and Education of Children of All Ages, Based on a Rediscovery of the True Principles and Vision of Maria Montessori*.
3 Several authors argue that beyond schooling, public media such as reality television (Ouellette 2007) and home gaming devices (Francombe 2010) have similar sorts of effects on individual's notions of self-control and valued corporeal practices that conform with gender stereotypes.

References

Almlund, Mathilde, Angela Lee Duckworth, James Heckman, and Tim Kautz. 2011. "Personality Psychology and Economics." In *Handbook of the Economics of Education*, 4: 1–181. Elsevier. http://linkinghub.elsevier.com/retrieve/pii/B9780444534446000018.

Au, Wayne. 2009. *Unequal by Design: High-Stakes Testing and the Standardization of Inequality*. New York; London: Routledge.

Ausdale, Debra Van, and Joe R. Feagin. 2001. *The First R: How Children Learn Race and Racism*. New York: Rowman & Littlefield.

Averett, Susan, and Korenman, Sanders. 1996. "The Economic Reality of The Beauty Myth." *The Journal of Human Resources* 31 (2): 304–30.

Bain, Linda L. 1985. "The Hidden Curriculum Re-Examined." *Quest* 37 (2): 145–53.

Barber, Benjamin R. 1994. *An Aristocracy of Everyone: The Politics of Education and the Future of America*, 1st edn. New York: Ballantine Books.

Bauer, Katherine W., Y. Wendy Yang, and S. Bryn Austin. 2004. "'How Can We Stay Healthy When You're Throwing All of This in Front of Us?' Findings from Focus Groups and Interviews in Middle Schools on Environmental Influences on Nutrition and Physical Activity." *Health Education & Behavior* 31 (1): 34–46. doi: 10.1177/1090198103255372.

Bernstein, Basil B. 1973. *Class, Codes and Control*. London: Routledge.

Binkley, Sam. 2011. "Happiness, Positive Psychology and the Program of Neoliberal Governmentality." *Subjectivity* 4 (4): 371–94.

Bomer, Randy, Joel Dworin, Laura May, and Peggy Semingson. 2008. "Miseducating Teachers about the Poor: A Critical Analysis of Ruby Payne's Claims about Poverty." *The Teachers College Record* 110 (12): 2497–531.

Bourdieu, Pierre. 1977. *Outline of a Theory of Practice*. Cambridge: Cambridge University Press.

Bourdieu, Pierre. 1984. *Distinction: A Social Critique of the Judgement of Taste*. Cambridge, MA: Harvard University Press.

Bourdieu, Pierre. 1990. *The Logic of Practice*. Stanford, CA: Stanford University Press.

Bourdieu, Pierre. 1991. *Language and Symbolic Power*. Cambridge, MA: Harvard University Press.

Bowey, Judith A. 1995. "Socioeconomic Status Differences in Preschool Phonological Sensitivity and First-Grade Reading Achievement." *Journal of Educational Psychology* 87 (3): 476–87. doi: 10.1037/0022-0663.87.3.476.

Bradley, Robert H., and Robert F. Corwyn. 2002. "Socioeconomic Status and Child Development." *Annual Review of Psychology* 53 (1): 371–99. doi: 10.1146/annurev.psych.53.100901.135233.

Brody, Howard, and Linda M. Hunt. 2006. "BiDil: Assessing a Race-Based Pharmaceutical." *Annals of Family Medicine* 4 (6): 556–60. doi: 10.1370/afm.582.

Brooks-Gunn, Jeanne, and Greg J. Duncan. 1997. "The Effects of Poverty on Children." *The Future of Children* 7 (2): 55–71.

Burgess, Norma J., and Eurnestine Brown. 1999. *African-American Women: An Ecological Perspective*. New York: Falmer Press.

Burke, Kenneth. 1969. *A Rhetoric of Motives*. Oakland, CA: University of California Press.

Butler, Judith. 1993. *Bodies That Matter. Routledge*. London: Routledge.

Butler, Judith. 2006. *Gender Trouble: Feminism and the Subversion of Identity (Routledge Classics)*, 1st edn. London: Routledge.

Caird, Jennifer, Josephine Kavanagh, Alison O'Mara-Eves, Kathryn Oliver, Sandy Oliver, Claire Stansfield, and James Thomas. 2013. "Does Being Overweight Impede Academic Attainment? A Systematic Review." *Health Education Journal*, June, 0017896913489289. doi: 10.1177/0017896913489289.

Calarco, Jessica McCrory. 2011. "'I Need Help!' Social Class and Children's Help-Seeking in Elementary School." *American Sociological Review* 76 (6): 862–82. doi: 10.1177/0003122411427177.

Carels, R. A., K. M. Young, C. B. Wott, J. Harper, A. Gumble, M. Wagner Hobbs, and A. M. Clayton. 2009. "Internalized Weight Stigma and Its Ideological Correlates Among Weight Loss Treatment Seeking Adults." *Eating and Weight Disorders : EWD* 14 (2–3): e92–e97.

Carr, Deborah, and Michael A. Friedman. 2005. "Is Obesity Stigmatizing? Body Weight, Perceived Discrimination, and Psychological Well-Being in the United States." *Journal of Health and Social Behavior* 46 (3): 244–59. doi: 10.1177/002214650504600303.

Carr, Sarah. 2013. *Hope Against Hope: Three Schools, One City, and the Struggle to Educate America's Children*. New York: Bloomsbury Publishing.

Cawley, John. 2004. "The Impact of Obesity on Wages." *The Journal of Human Resources* XXXIX (2): 451–74.

Cohen, Sheldon, Cuneyt M. Alper, William J. Doyle, Nancy Adler, John J. Treanor, and Ronald B. Turner. 2008. "Objective and Subjective Socioeconomic Status and Susceptibility to the Common Cold." *Health Psychology* 27 (2): 268–74. doi: 10.1037/0278–6133.27.2.268.

Cole, Luella. 1939. "Instruction in Penmanship for the Left-Handed Child." *The Elementary School Journal* 39 (6): 436–48. doi: 10.2307/997703.

Conley, Dalton, and Rebecca Glauber. 2005. "Gender, Body Mass and Economic Status." Working Paper 11343. National Bureau of Economic Research. http://www.nber.org/papers/w11343.

Cooley, Charles Horton. 1992. *Human Nature and the Social Order*. Transaction Publishers.

Cregan, Kate. 2006. *The Sociology of the Body: Mapping the Abstraction of Embodiment*. London: SAGE.

Crocker, Jennifer, Beth Cornwell, and Brenda Major. 1993. "The Stigma of Overweight: Affective Consequences of Attributional Ambiguity." *Journal of Personality and Social Psychology* 64 (1): 60–70. doi: 10.1037/0022–3514.64.1.60.

Datar, Ashlesha, and Roland Sturm. 2006. "Childhood Overweight and Elementary School Outcomes." *International Journal of Obesity (2005)* 30 (9): 1449–60. doi: 10.1038/sj.ijo.0803311.

Davis, Lennard J. 1995. *Enforcing Normalcy: Disability, Deafness, and the Body*. London; New York: Verso.

Davis, Lennard J., and Michael F. Bérubé. 2002. *Bending Over Backwards: Disability, Dismodernism and Other Difficult Positions*, 1st edn. New York: New York University Press.

Deleuze, Gilles, Felix Guattari, and Brian Massumi. 1987. *A Thousand Plateaus: Capitalism and Schizophrenia*, 1st edn. Minneapolis: University of Minnesota Press.

Delpit, Lisa D. 1988. "The Silenced Dialogue: Power and Pedagogy in Educating Other People's Children." *Harvard Educational Review* 58 (3): 280–99.

Demuth, A., U. Czerniak, and E. Ziółkowska-Łajp. 2013. "A Comparison of a Subjective Body Assessment of Men and Women of the Polish Social Elite." *HOMO--Journal of Comparative Human Biology* 64 (5): 398–409. doi: 10.1016/j.jchb.2013.07.001.

Dewey, John. 2007. *Experience And Education*. New York: Simon and Schuster.

Domhoff, G. William. 2013. *Who Rules America? The Triumph of the Corporate Rich*, 7th edn. New York: McGraw-Hill Humanities/Social Sciences/Languages.

Downey, Douglas B., Paul T. von Hippel, and Beckett A. Broh. 2004. "Are Schools the Great Equalizer? Cognitive Inequality during the Summer Months and the School Year." *American Sociological Review* 69 (5): 613–35. doi: 10.1177/000312240406900501.

Duckworth, Angela Lee, and Martin E. P. Seligman. 2005. "Self-Discipline Outdoes IQ in Predicting Academic Performance of Adolescents." *Psychological Science* 16 (12): 939–44. doi: 10.1111/j.1467-9280.2005.01641.x.

Duckworth, Angela Lee, Patrick D. Quinn, and Martin E. P. Seligman. 2009. "Positive Predictors of Teacher Effectiveness." *The Journal of Positive Psychology* 4 (6): 540–47. doi: 10.1080/17439760903157232.

Duncan, Greg J., Johanne Boisjoly, and Kathleen Mullan Harris. 2001. "Sibling, Peer, Neighbor, and Schoolmate Correlations as Indicators of the Importance of Context for Adolescent Development." *Demography* 38 (3): 437–47. doi: 10.1353/dem.2001.0026.

Ellison, Scott. 2012. "It's in the Name: A Synthetic Inquiry of the Knowledge Is Power Program [KIPP]." *Educational Studies* 48 (6): 550–75. doi: 10.1080/00131946.2011.647156.

Escobar, Arturo. 2007. "The 'Ontological Turn' in Social Theory. A Commentary on 'Human Geography without Scale', by Sallie Marston, John Paul Jones II and Keith Woodward." *Transactions of the Institute of British Geographers* 32 (1): 106–11. doi: 10.1111/j.1475-5661.2007.00243.x.

Farnell, Brenda. 2000. "Getting out of the Habitus: An Alternative Model of Dynamically Embodied Social Action." *Journal of the Royal Anthropological Institute* 6 (3): 397–418. doi: 10.1111/1467-9655.00023.

Farrell, Amy Erdman. 2011. *Fat Shame: Stigma and the Fat Body in American Culture*. New York: New York University Press.

Featherstone, Mike, Mike Hepworth, and Bryan S. Turner. 1991. *The Body: Social Process and Cultural Theory*. Thousand Oaks, CA: SAGE.

Fleming, Christina. 2010. "Dave Levin, Co-Founder of KIPP, Delivers the First Keynote." *Columbia Journalism School*. http://www.journalism.columbia.edu/page/642/425.

Fournier, Marcel. 2006. *Marcel Mauss: A Biography*. Princeton, NJ: Princeton University Press.

Francombe, Jessica. 2010. "'I Cheer, You Cheer, We Cheer': Physical Technologies and the Normalized Body." *Television & New Media* 11 (5): 350–66. doi: 10.1177/1527476410363483.

Friedlander Sheila L., Emma K. Larkin, Carol L. Rosen, Tonya M. Palermo, and Susan Redline. 2003. "Decreased Quality of Life Associated with Obesity in School-Aged Children." *Archives of Pediatrics & Adolescent Medicine* 157 (12): 1206–11. doi: 10.1001/archpedi.157.12.1206.

Giroux, Henry A. 2001. *Theory and Resistance in Education: Towards a Pedagogy for the Opposition, Revised and Expanded Edition (Critical Studies in Education and Culture Series)*. New York: Praeger.

Gorski, Paul C. 2006. ID Number: 12322. "The Classist Underpinnings of Ruby Payne's Framework." Teachers College Record, Date Published: February 09, 2006 Http://www.tcrecord.org ID Number: 12322, Accessed: February 10, 2013 3:24:39 PM.

"Graphic: How Class Works—New York Times." 2014. Accessed February 20. http://www.nytimes.com/packages/html/national/20050515_CLASS_GRAPHIC/index_04.html.

Greenleaf, Christy, and Karen Weiller. 2005. "Perceptions of Youth Obesity among Physical Educators." *Social Psychology of Education* 8 (4): 407–23. doi: 10.1007/s11218-005-0662-9.

"Habitus, N." 2013. *OED Online*. Oxford University Press. Accessed December 6. http://www.oed.com/view/Entry/83009.

Hackman, Daniel A., Martha J. Farah, and Michael J. Meaney. 2010. "Socioeconomic Status and the Brain: Mechanistic Insights from Human and Animal Research." *Nature Reviews Neuroscience* 11 (9): 651–59. doi: 10.1038/nrn2897.

Hart, Betty, and Todd R. Risley. 1995. *Meaningful Differences in the Everyday Experience of Young American Children*, Vol. xxiii. Baltimore, MD, US; Paul H Brookes Publishing.

Harvey, David. 2007. *A Brief History of Neoliberalism*. Oxford; New York: Oxford University Press.

Hays, Sharon. 1996. *The Cultural Contradictions of Motherhood*. New Haven: Yale University Press.

Heath, Shirley Brice. 1983. *Ways with Words: Language, Life and Work in Communities and Classrooms*. Cambridge: Cambridge University Press.

Heckman, James J. 1999. "Policies to Foster Human Capital." Working Paper 7288. National Bureau of Economic Research. http://www.nber.org/papers/w7288.

Henry, Sue Ellen. 2005. "'I Can Never Turn My Back On That': Liminality and the Impact of Social Class on Service Learning Experience.'" In *Looking In, Teaching Out: Critical Issues and Directions in Service-Learning*. New York: Palgrave Press.

Henry, Sue Ellen. 2013. "Bodies at Home and at School: Toward a Theory of Embodied Social Class Status." *Educational Theory* 63 (1): 1–16. doi: 10.1111/edth.12006.

Herrnstein, Richard J., and Charles Murray. 1996. *Bell Curve: Intelligence and Class Structure in American Life*. New York: Free Press.

Hertz, Tom. 2006. "Understanding Mobility in America." *Center for American Progress Discussion Paper*. http://citeseerx.ist.psu.edu/viewdoc/download?doi=10.1.1.107.5196&rep=rep1&type=pdf.

Hobson, Janell. 2012. *Body as Evidence Mediating Race, Globalizing Gender*. Albany, NY: SUNY Press.

Holloway, Karla F. C. 2011. *Private Bodies, Public Texts: Race, Gender, and a Cultural Bioethics*. Durham, NC: Duke University Press.

Holt, Louise. 2004. "Children with Mind–body Differences: Performing Disability in Primary School Classrooms." *Children's Geographies* 2 (2): 219–36. doi: 10.1080/1473328041000172052o.

Horn, Jim. 2010. "Corporatism, KIPP, and Cultural Eugenics." In *The Gates Foundation and the Future of US "Public" Schools* (*Routledge Studies in Education and Neoliberalism*), 1st edn, 80–103. London: Routledge.

Inda, Jonathan Xavier. 2013. "For Blacks Only: Pharmaceuticals, Genetics, and the Racial Politics of Life." Accessed September 20. http://www.academia.edu/2517586/For_Blacks_Only_Pharmaceuticals_Genetics_and_the_Racial_Politics_of_Life.

Isaacs, Julia B. 2014. "Economic Mobility of Families Across Generations." *The Brookings Institution*. Accessed March 4. http://www.brookings.edu/research/papers/2007/11/generations-isaacs.

James, Allison. 1993. *Childhood Identities: Self and Social Relationships in the Experience of the Child*. Edinburgh: Edinburgh University Press.

James, Allison. 2000. "Embodied Being(s): Understanding the Self and the Body in Childhood." In *The Body, Childhood and Society*, edited by Alan Prout, 19–38. New York: St. Martin's Press.

Jensen, Arthur. 1969. "How Much Can We Boost IQ and Scholastic Achievement?" *Harvard Educational Review* 39 (1): 1–123.

Jensen, Arthur. 1973. "The Differences Are Real." *Psychology Today*, December.

Jones, Alison. 2000. "Surveillance and Student Handwriting: Tracing the Body." In *Taught Bodies*, edited by Clare O'Farrell, Daphne Meadmore, Erica McWilliam, and Colin Symes, 151–65. New York: Peter Lang.

Kaestner, Robert, and Michael Grossman. 2009. "Effects of Weight on Children's Educational Achievement." *Economics of Education Review* 28 (6): 651–61. doi: 10.1016/j.econedurev.2009.03.002.

Kasser, Tim, Steve Cohn, Allen D. Kanner, and Richard M. Ryan. 2007. "Some Costs of American Corporate Capitalism: A Psychological Exploration of Value and Goal Conflicts." *Psychological Inquiry* 18 (1): 1–22.

Katz, Cindi. 2004. *Growing Up Global: Economic Restructuring and Children's Everyday Lives*. Minneapolis: University of Minnesota Press.

Kerry S. O'Brien, John A. Hunter, and M Banks. 2007. "Implicit Anti-Fat Bias in Physical Educators: Physical Attributes, Ideology and Socialization." *International Journal of Obesity (2005)* 31 (2): 308–14. doi: 10.1038/sj.ijo.0803398.

Kim, Pilyoung, Gary W. Evans, Michael Angstadt, S. Shaun Ho, Chandra S. Sripada, James E. Swain, Israel Liberzon, and K. Luan Phan. 2013. "Effects of Childhood Poverty and Chronic Stress on Emotion Regulatory Brain Function in Adulthood." *Proceedings of the National Academy of Sciences*, October, 201308240. doi: 10.1073/pnas.1308240110.

Kingston, Paul W. 2000. *The Classless Society*. Stanford, CA: Stanford University Press.

Kramer, Rita. 1988. *Maria Montessori: A Biography (Radcliffe Biography Series)*. Boston: Da Capo Press.

Kraus, Michael W., Stéphane Côté, and Dacher Keltner. 2010. "Social Class, Contextualism, and Empathic Accuracy." *Psychological Science* 21 (11): 1716–23. doi: 10.1177/0956797610387613.

Kraus, Michael W., and Dacher Keltner. 2009. "Signs of Socioeconomic Status A Thin-Slicing Approach." *Psychological Science* 20 (1): 99–106. doi: 10.1111/j.1467-9280.2008.02251.x.

Kraus, Michael W., Paul K. Piff, and Dacher Keltner. 2011. "Social Class as Culture The Convergence of Resources and Rank in the Social Realm." *Current Directions in Psychological Science* 20 (4): 246–50. doi: 10.1177/0963721411414654.
Laflamme, Lucie, Marie Hasselberg, and Stephanie Burrows. 2010. "20 Years of Research on Socioeconomic Inequality and Children: Unintentional Injuries Understanding the Cause-Specific Evidence at Hand." *International Journal of Pediatrics* 2010 (July). doi: 10.1155/2010/819687. http://www.hindawi.com/journals/ijped/2010/819687/abs/.
Lareau, Annette. 2003 and 2011. *Unequal Childhoods: Class, Race and Family Life*. Oakland: University of California Press.
Lee, Valerie E., and David T. Burkam. 2002. "Inequality at the Starting Gate: Social Background Differences in Achievement as Children Begin School." January. http://eric.ed.gov/?id=ED470551.
Lewis, Catherine C. 1995. *Educating Hearts and Minds: Reflections on Japanese Preschool and Elementary Education*, 1st edn. Cambridge: Cambridge University Press.
Lewis, Oscar. 1963. "The Culture of Poverty." *Trans-Action* 1 (1): 17–19. doi: 10.1007/BF03182237.
———. 1975. *Five Families: Mexican Case Studies in the Culture of Poverty*. Basic Books.
MacLeod, Jay. 2008. *Ain't No Makin' It: Aspirations and Attainment in a Low-Income Neighborhood*, 3rd edn. Boulder, CO: Westview Press.
Mason, Katherine. 2013. "Social Stratification and the Body: Gender, Race, and Class." *Sociology Compass* 7 (8): 686–98.
"Massachusetts Teachers Aim To Knock Down 'Data Walls.'" 2014. *Truthout*. Accessed February 14. http://truth-out.org/news/item/21861-massachusetts-teachers-aim-to-knock-down-data-walls.
Massey, Douglas S. 1996. "The Age of Extremes: Concentrated Affluence and Poverty in the Twenty-First Century." *Demography* 33 (4): 395–412. doi: 10.2307/2061773.
Mcginnis Gonzalez, Sherri. 2013. "Growing up Poor and Stressed Impacts Brain Function as an Adult." *Medical Xpress*, October 21. http://medicalxpress.com/news/2013-10-poor-stressed-impacts-brain-function.html.
McGregor, Glenda. 2009. "Educating for (whose) Success? Schooling in an Age of Neo-Liberalism." *British Journal of Sociology of Education* 30 (3): 345–58.

McLanahan, Sara. 2004. "Diverging Destinies: How Children Are Faring under the Second Demographic Transition." *Demography* 41 (4): 607–27. doi: 10.1353/dem.2004.0033.

Montessori, Maria. 1964. *The Montessori Method*. New York: Random House.

Musher-Eizenman, Dara R., Shayla C. Holub, Amy Barnhart Miller, Sara E. Goldstein, and Laura Edwards-Leeper. 2004. "Body Size Stigmatization in Preschool Children: The Role of Control Attributions." *Journal of Pediatric Psychology* 29 (8): 613–20. doi: 10.1093/jpepsy/jsh063.

National Poverty Center. 2004. "Substance Abuse and Welfare Reform." Policy Brief #2.

Navarro, Vicente. 1991. "Race *or* Class or Race *and* Class: Growing Mortality Differentials in the United States." *International Journal of Health Services* 21 (2): 229–35. doi: 10.2190/5WXM-QK9K-PTMQ-T1FG.

Nelson, Margaret K., and Rebecca Schutz. 2007. "Day Care Differences and the Reproduction of Social Class." *Journal of Contemporary Ethnography* 36 (3): 281–317. doi: 10.1177/0891241606293137.

Nespor, Jan. 1987. "The Role of Beliefs in the Practice of Teaching." *Journal of Curriculum Studies* 19 (4): 317–28. doi: 10.1080/0022027870190403.

Neumark-Sztainer, Dianne, Mary Story, and Tanya Harris. 1999. "Beliefs and Attitudes about Obesity among Teachers and School Health Care Providers Working with Adolescents." *Journal of Nutrition Education* 31 (1): 3–9. doi: 10.1016/S0022-3182(99)70378-X.

Ng, Jennifer C., and John L Rury. 2006. "Poverty and Education: A Critical Analysis of the Ruby Payne Phenomenon." *Teachers College Record*, July. http://www.tcrecord.org ID number: 12596.

Noland, Carrie. 2010. *Agency and Embodiment: Performing Gestures/Producing Culture*. Cambridge, MA: Harvard University Press.

Ogden, Cynthia L., Margaret D. Carroll, Brian K. Kit, and Katherine M. Flegal. 2012. "Prevalence of Obesity and Trends in Body Mass Index among US Children and Adolescents, 1999–2010." *JAMA: The Journal of the American Medical Association* 307 (5): 483–90. doi: 10.1001/jama.2012.40.

Organization of Economic Co-operation and Development. 2011. "Towards an OECD Skills Strategy." Paris: OECD. http://www.oecd.org/edu/47769000.pdf.

Ouellette, Laurie. 2007. "'Take Reponsibility for Yourself': Judge Judy and the Neoliberal Citizen." In *Feminist Television Criticism: A Reader*, 370. Columbus, OH: McGraw-Hill International.

Payne, Ruby K. 2005. *A Framework for Understanding Poverty*, 4th edn. Highlands TX: Aha! Process, Inc.

Payne, Ruby K., Philip E. DeVol, and Terie Dreussi Smith. 2006. *Bridges out of Poverty: Strategies for Professionals and Communities*. Highlands, TX: Aha! Process.

Peterson, Christopher, and Martin E. P. Seligman. 2004. *Character Strengths and Virtues: A Handbook and Classification*. Washington, DC New York: American Psychological Association.

Pingitore, Regina, Bernard L. Dugoni, R. Scott Tindale, and Bonnie Spring. 1994. "Bias against Overweight Job Applicants in a Simulated Employment Interview." *Journal of Applied Psychology* 79 (6): 909–17. doi: 10.1037/0021-9010.79.6.909.

Puhl, Rebecca M., and Chelsea A. Heuer. 2009. "The Stigma of Obesity: A Review and Update." *Obesity* 17 (5): 941–64. doi: 10.1038/oby.2008.636.

Reardon, Sean. 2011. "The Widening Academic Achievement Gap Between the Rich and the Poor: New Evidence and Possible Explanations." In *Wither Opportunity? Rising Inequality, Schools and Children's Life Chances*, edited by Greg J. Duncan, and Richard J. Murnane. New York:Russell Sage Foundation.

"Report on Discriminiation due to Physical Size." 1994. Washington, DC: National Education Association.

Ridgeway, Cecilia L. 2014. "Why Status Matters for Inequality." *American Sociological Review* 79 (1): 1–16.

Rist, Ray C. 1970. "Student Social Class and Teacher Expectations: The Self-Fulfilling Prophecy in Ghetto Education." *Harvard Educational Review* 40 (3): 411–451.

Rist, Ray C. 2000. "HER Classic: Student Social Class and Teacher Expectations: The Self-Fulfilling Prophecy in Ghetto Education." *Harvard Educational Review* 70 (3): 257–301.

Rothblum, Esther, and Sondra Solovay. 2009. *The Fat Studies Reader*. New York: New York University Press.

Sacker, Amanda, Ingrid Schoon, and Mel Bartley. 2002. "Social Inequality in Educational Achievement and Psychosocial Adjustment throughout Childhood: Magnitude and Mechanisms." *Social Science & Medicine* 55 (5): 863–80. doi: 10.1016/S0277-9536(01)00228-3.

Sackrey, Charles, Geoffrey Eugene Schneider, Janet T Knoedler, and Hans Jensen. 2010. *Introduction to Political Economy*. Boston, MA: Dollars and Sense, Economic Affairs Bureau.

Sankar, Pamela. 2005. "BiDil: Race Medicine Or Race Marketing?" *Health Affairs*, October. doi: 10.1377/hlthaff.w5.455. http://content.healthaffairs.org/cgi/doi/10.1377/hlthaff.w5.455.

Scott, Janny. 2005. "Life at the Top in America Isn't Just Better, It's Longer." *New York Times*, A1.

Sherman, Jennifer, and Elizabeth Harris. 2012. "Social Class and Parenting: Classic Debates and New Understandings." *Sociology Compass* 6 (1): 60–71. doi: 10.1111/j.1751-9020.2011.00430.x.

Shilling, Chris. 1997. "The Undersocialised Conception of the Embodied Agent in Modern Sociology." *Sociology* 31 (4): 737–54. doi: 10.1177/0038038597031004006.

Shilling, Chris. 2003. *The Body and Social Theory*. London; Thousand Oaks, CA: SAGE. http://site.ebrary.com/id/10326960.

Shilling, Chris. 2010. "Exploring the Society-Body-School Nexus: Theoretical and Methodology Issues in the Study of Body Pedagogics." *Sport, Education and Society* 15 (2): 151–67.

Shuffelton, Amy B. 2013. "A Matter of Friendship: Educational Interventions into Culture and Poverty." *Educational Theory* 63 (3): 299–316. doi: 10.1111/edth.12025.

Sirin, Selcuk R. 2005. "Socioeconomic Status and Academic Achievement: A Meta-Analytic Review of Research." *Review of Educational Research* 75 (3): 417–53. doi: 10.3102/00346543075003417.

Skattebol, Jennifer. 2006. "Playing Boys: The Body, Identity and Belonging in the Early Years." *Gender and Education* 18 (5): 507–22. doi: 10.1080/09540250600881667.

Skeggs, Beverley. 2004. *Class, Self, Culture*. London: Routledge.

———. 2005. "The Making of Class and Gender through Visualizing Moral Subject Formation." *Sociology* 39 (5): 965–82. doi: 10.1177/0038038505058381.

Sparks, Sarah D. 2013. "Study Finds 'No Place to Get Away' From Deep Poverty in South, West Schools." *Education Week—Inside School Research*. October 21. http://blogs.edweek.org/edweek/inside-school-research/2013/10/theres_no_place_you_can_get_aw.html?cmp=SOC-SHR-FB.

Stiglitz, Joseph E. 2013. *The Price of Inequality: How Today's Divided Society Endangers Our Future*, 1st edn. W. W. Norton & Company.

Stipek, Deborah J. 1993. "Motivation To Learn: From Theory to Practice. Second Edition." January. http://eric.ed.gov/?id=ED369773.

Stipek, Deborah, and Heidi J. Gralinski. 1996. "Children's Beliefs about Intelligence and School Performance." *Journal of Educational Psychology* 88 (3): 397–407. doi: 10.1037/0022-0663.88.3.397.

Stipek, Deborah J., and Rosaleen H. Ryan. 1997. "Economically Disadvantaged Preschoolers: Ready to Learn but Further to Go." *Developmental Psychology* 33 (4): 711–23. doi: 10.1037/0012-1649.33.4.711.

Stitzlein, Sarah Marie. 2008. *Breaking Bad Habits of Race and Gender: Transforming Identity in Schools*. New York: Rowman & Littlefield Publishers.

Storch, Eric A., Vanessa A. Milsom, Ninoska DeBraganza, Adam B. Lewin, Gary R. Geffken, and Janet H. Silverstein. 2007. "Peer Victimization, Psychosocial Adjustment, and Physical Activity in Overweight and At-Risk-For-Overweight Youth." *Journal of Pediatric Psychology* 32 (1): 80–89. doi: 10.1093/jpepsy/jsj113.

Strauss, Richard S. 2000. "Childhood Obesity and Self-Esteem." *Pediatrics* 105 (1): e15–e15.

Thayer-Bacon, Barbara. 2012. "Maria Montessori, John Dewey, and William H. Kilpatrick." *Education and Culture* 28 (1): 3–20. doi: 10.1353/eac.2012.0001.

The Pew Charitable Trusts. 2014. "Economic Mobility Project." Accessed March 4. http://www.pewstates.org/projects/economic-mobility-project-328061.

Thernstrom, Abigail M., and Stephen Thernstrom. 2003. *No Excuses: Closing the Racial Gap in Learning*. New York: Simon & Schuster.

Thomson, Rosemarie Garland. 1996. *Extraordinary Bodies: Figuring Physical Disability in American Culture and Literature*, 1st edn. New York: Columbia University Press.

Tobin, Joseph. 2004. "The Disappearance of The Body in Early Childhood Education." In *Knowing Bodies, Moving Minds*, edited by Liora Bresler, 111–27. The Netherlands: Kluver Academic Publishers.

Tobin, Joseph J., David Y. H. Wu, and Dana H. Davidson. 1991. *Preschool in Three Cultures: Japan, China and the United States*. Yale University Press.

Tough, Paul. 2012. *How Children Succeed: Grit, Curiosity, and the Hidden Power of Character*. New York: Houghton Mifflin Harcourt.

Valencia, Richard R. 1997. *The Evolution of Deficit Thinking: Educational Thought and Practice*. Florence, KY: Psychology Press.

Walkerdine, Valerie. 1990. *Schoolgirl Fictions*. New York: Verso.

Walker, Dale, Charles Greenwood, Betty Hart, and Judith Carta. 1994. "Prediction of School Outcomes Based on Early Language

Production and Socioeconomic Factors." *Child Development* 65 (2): 606–21. doi: 10.1111/j.1467-8624.1994.tb00771.x.

Walker, Susan P., Theodore D. Wachs, Sally Grantham-McGregor, Maureen M. Black, Charles A. Nelson, Sandra L. Huffman, Helen Baker-Henningham, Susan M. Chang, Jena D. Hamadani, and Betsy Lozoff. 2011. "Inequality in Early Childhood: Risk and Protective Factors for Early Child Development." *The Lancet* 378 (9799): 1325–38.

Watkins, Megan. 2012. *Discipline and Learn: Bodies, Pedagogy and Writing*. New York: Springer.

Weis, Lois, Cameron McCarthy, and Greg Dimitriadis. 2006. *Ideology, Curriculum, and the New Sociology of Education: Revisiting the Work of Michael Apple*. New York: Routledge.

Wentworth, Roland A. Lubie, and Felix Wentworth. 2013. *Montessori for the New Millennium: Practical Guidance on the Teaching and Education of Children of All Ages, Based on A Rediscovery of the True Principles and Vision of Maria Montessori*. London: Routledge.

Westbrook, Robert Brett. 1991. *John Dewey and American Democracy*. Ithaca, NY: Cornell University Press.

"What Matters Most: Teaching for America's Future: Report of the National Commission on Teaching & America's Future: Summary Report." 1996. National Commission on Teaching & America's Future (US).

Wilkinson, Richard G. 2006. *The Impact of Inequality: How to Make Sick Societies Healthier*, 1st edn. New York: The New Press.

Wilkinson, Richard G., and Kate E. Pickett. 2006. "Income Inequality and Population Health: A Review and Explanation of the Evidence." *Social Science & Medicine* 62 (7): 1768–84. doi: 10.1016/j.socscimed.2005.08.036.

Williams, David R., Mark B. McClellan, and Alice M. Rivlin. 2010. "Beyond The Affordable Care Act: Achieving Real Improvements In Americans' Health." *Health Affairs* 29 (8): 1481–88. doi: 10.1377/hlthaff.2010.0071.

Yoo, Joan P., Kristen S. Slack, and Jane L. Holl. 2009. "Material Hardship and the Physical Health of School-Aged Children in Low-Income Households." *American Journal of Public Health* 99 (5): 829–36. doi: 10.2105/AJPH.2007.119776.

Zavodny, Madeline. 2013. "Does Weight Affect Children's Test Scores and Teacher Assessments Differently?" *Economics of Education Review* 34 (June): 135–45. doi: 10.1016/j.econedurev.2013.02.003.

Index

absent-presence, 55
abstraction, 20, 110
academic achievement
  overweight children, 30
accomplishment of natural
    growth, 74
  advantages, 79
  consequences for children,
    78
  personal decision making,
    100
achievement gap, 94, 112
achievement ideology, 99
agency, 112
  corporeal, 52
  positive identity, 51
  resistance, 42
  use of the body, 45
Annette Lareau, 9
Arthur Jensen, 31
assemblages, 11

Basil Bernstein, 9
BiDil, 32
bi-directional approach, 25
  study of social class and the
    body, 25
biological determinism
  of self-control, 31
bodily comportment
  KIPP, 93, 95, 97, 109
body, 12
  absent presence, 18
  addiction assertions in
    Payne, 87

body hexis communication,
    66
children's agency, 16
  disappearing, 103
  historical study of, 55
  identity, 47
  impediment to thinking,
    17
  influence on social class, 27
  lessons about, 17
  race and personality, 31
  reciprocal relationship with
    society, 56
  social class influences on, 33
  social norms, 57
Body hexis, 7
  definition, 66

capital
  caveats about, 65
  forms of, 64
Carrie Noland, 42
Catherine Lewis, 104, 106
Charles Cooley, 28
childhood obesity, 28
child-rearing
  logics of, 70
children's agency, 48
  categorical identity, 47
co-constitutive, 25
  children's identities, 47
  orientation to embodiment,
    43
  study of social class and the
    body, 25

comportment
    teacher-imposed, 95
concerted cultivation, 70, 91
    advantages to, 72
    disadvantages, 73
    judgment and negotiation, 100
consumer
    neoliberal conception of citizen, 109
corporeal
    habits at KIPP, 96
    Ruby Payne, 88
corporeal control
    and lack of self-control, 105
corporeal expectations
    and symbolic violence, 110
corporeal norms
    middle class, 95
cultural-interventionist, 113

(dis)ability, 52
Disability Studies, 39
discrimination, 27
    against overweight children, 29
    gender, 28
dualisms
    mind/body, 47

embodied, 68
embodied knowledge, 15
embodiment, 11, 100
Emile Durkheim, 56

Fat Studies, 39
Field, 62

genki
    in Japanese elementary classrooms, 106
goals
    of Japanese elementary classrooms, 106

habits
    in Mauss, 59
Habitus, 7
    according to Bourdieu, 61
    and body hexis, 66
    concealment, 63
    critique of, 61
    relationship to field, 62
    shaping beliefs, 63
    social facts, 59
    vs. habits, 61
handedness, 40
Healthy at any Size, 39
hidden rules
    of school, 88

John Dewey, 41, 104
Joseph Tobin, 108

Knowledge is Power Program (KIPP), 92, 109, 112
    5 pillars, 94
    goal, 93
    outcomes, 98
    required corporeal performances in, 99

language differences
    and social class, 9
Lareau
    parenting logics, 10
learned helplessness, 94
liberal self
    neoliberal rhetoric, 111
liberty
    in Montessori's philosophy, 104
    vs. conformity, 108
lockdown, 98

Marcel Mauss, 55, 57
Martin Seligman, 93
Material differences, 34
Megan Watkins, 102

neoliberalism, 111
    influence on education, 18
    abstraction, 109
no excuses, 94, 100
non-normative bodies
    stereotypes of, 39
nonverbal communication, 10

ontological turn, 11
othering
   identity, 47

parenting practices
   social class differences, 8
Paulo Freire, 90
Positive Psychology, 93, 99, 111
   character education at KIPP, 93
poverty, 38
   childhood mortality, 35
   neurological differences, 36
procedural memory, 89
Protestant Work Ethic, 32
   and KIPP, 101

racism
   in children, 51
Ruby Payne, 85, 86, 109
   truth claims, 86

school rules, 82
self-advocacy, 91, 101
Self-control, 16, 81, 85, 101, 102, 104, 109–111, 113
   absence of, 16
   agency, 41
   and addiction, 87
   and social reproduction, 112
   and workplace discretion, 34
   compliance, 41
   corporeal, 16
   in Japanese elementary classrooms, 107
   KIPP conception, 99
   lack of, 32
   Montessori, 104
   neoliberal orientation, 105
   orientations to, 26
   overweight status, 28
   Ruby Payne, 91
   source of inequality, 33
   teacher demands for, 17
   weight, 32
self-fulfilling prophecies, 12
self-governance
   Montessori, 105
self-management, 107
SLANT
   KIPP classroom management, 94
Social class, 8, 113
   absence of, 6
   adult communication of, 67
   and body hexis, 7
   and the body, 25
   as an identity marker, 5
   cognitive differences, 37
   corporeal consequences, 36
   corporeal performance, 12, 52
   correlation with physical health, 33
   curricular influences, 85
   embodied, 53
   malleability of, 32
   power of, 5
   school readiness, 38
   self-evaluation, 7
   teacher perceptions of, 13
social mobility
   meritocracy, 5
social reproduction, 7, 110
socioeconomic status, 6
stereotypes
   held by teachers, 29
   Ruby Payne, 89
symbolic violence, 110

Techniques of the Body, 57–59

working-class, 91

GPSR Compliance

The European Union's (EU) General Product Safety Regulation (GPSR) is a set of rules that requires consumer products to be safe and our obligations to ensure this.

If you have any concerns about our products, you can contact us on

ProductSafety@springernature.com

In case Publisher is established outside the EU, the EU authorized representative is:

Springer Nature Customer Service Center GmbH
Europaplatz 3
69115 Heidelberg, Germany

www.ingramcontent.com/pod-product-compliance
Lightning Source LLC
LaVergne TN
LVHW041956060526
838200LV00002B/34

BRIGHT NOTES

THE PRINCE AND OTHER WORKS BY NICCOLÒ MACHIAVELLI

Intelligent Education

Nashville, Tennessee

BRIGHT NOTES: The Prince and Other Works
www.BrightNotes.com

No part of this publication may be used or reproduced in any manner whatsoever without written permission, except in the case of brief quotations in critical articles and reviews. For permissions, contact Influence Publishers http://www.influencepublishers.com.

ISBN: 978-1-645423-54-6 (Paperback)
ISBN: 978-1-645423-55-3 (eBook)

Published in accordance with the U.S. Copyright Office Orphan Works and Mass Digitization report of the register of copyrights, June 2015.

Originally published by Monarch Press.
Robert Sobel; Laurie Rozakis, 1965
2020 Edition published by Influence Publishers.

Interior design by Lapiz Digital Services. Cover Design by Thinkpen Designs.

Printed in the United States of America.

Library of Congress Cataloging-in-Publication Data forthcoming.
Names: Intelligent Education
Title: BRIGHT NOTES: The Prince and Other Works
Subject: STU004000 STUDY AIDS / Book Notes